JB
still

ONE DAY, LEVIN...
HE BE FREE

ONE DAY, LEVIN...
HE BE FREE

WILLIAM STILL AND THE
UNDERGROUND RAILROAD

BY

LUREY KHAN

E. P. DUTTON & CO., INC.   NEW YORK

Published simultaneously in Canada by Clarke,
Irwin & Company Limited, Toronto and Vancouver

SBN: 0–525–36415–3   LCC: 76–179057

Designed by Hilda Scott
Printed in the U.S.A.
First Edition

To the memory of Levin Still
and to all those
who have longed to be free,
and to my mother, Mabel Smith Khan,
a granddaughter of James Still

PUBLISHER'S NOTE

Most extracts in *One Day, Levin . . . He Be Free* are from *The Underground Rail Road* by William Still, published by Porter and Coates in Philadelphia in 1872. This book was out of print for many years but is now available in some libraries in a reprint edition published by Arno Press, New York, 1968.

An annotated bibliography giving the source of other material used by the author is on page 231.

Engravings and photographs from the time appear on pages 32–42 and 180–186.

chapter one

Levin and Sidney Steel were both slaves on the eastern shore of Maryland. Sidney, the wife, was a well-built black woman, young and beautiful; Levin, the husband, was muscular and powerful, a field hand who walked with an erect and proud carriage, suggesting above all that he was his own man. Because of his "uppity airs" the overseer informed Levin's owner, Saunders Griffin, that the young slave bore watching.

The slave master met his bondsman face to face and asked him why he did not shuffle and walk with his eyes cast to the ground, as was the custom with slaves.

Levin managed to withhold his anger while he answered.

"I cain't rightly tell why, Massa."

"Most of my slaves are happy here working the land," added the young slave master. "Why aren't you, Levin?"

Unable to restrain himself, the young black man unleashed his anger.

"I will die before I submit to the yoke!"

Enraged himself now, at this reply, Saunders Griffin, not yet twenty-one, glared at his slave, who was his very same age.

"You forget you are my slave, Levin!" he snapped.

"I cain't forget I is a slave!"

Then Griffin asked, "Levin, would you like to buy your freedom?"

The slave stood dumfounded at the offer! Gathering his wits about him, he gained enough presence of mind to mumble, "Massa know I do."

"Work about the place. Chores go begging every day. I will pay you for 'over-work.'"

Pausing, Levin asked: "What of Sidney and the boys?"

The planter hesitated. "I speak of your freedom, Levin. I need the boys to work here. Sidney must raise them."

Awestruck, the plowman dropped his head in despair.

"Go, Levin. Think about my offer. I know you will be glad to be free."

With those words, Griffin mounted his horse and rode to the stable by the great house where the white folks lived; and the young slave walked down to the cabins in the slave quarter.

Feigning joy, he rushed into the shack. His wife spooned hominy onto their children's plates as they sat at the pine table next to the hearth.

"Sidney, wife!" he said, "Massa tells me I be free!"

"I declare you been at Massa's cider," she replied with a smile.

The children ate greedily, but their parents walked out into the grove to talk over the events of the afternoon.

"If I hears it right, Levin," Sidney said, "Massa gonna give you free papers when you earns the money?"

"He swears it, wife! One day I be free!"

"An' Peter an' Levin? An' me?"

He turned his back to her and moved to the trunk of a giant evergreen.

2

"I will come back for you. For you all. God knows I promise to."

Sidney fought tears. She spoke calmly. "I reckon it gonna take a heap of time before you gets the money saved. Ain't no sense in frettin' now. The Lord, he will set things right."

His spirits brighter now, her husband held her close to him. "We's gonna face it when it come."

He hugged her and they both laughed softly. Then they walked hand in hand toward their cabin.

The years passed quickly. Levin worked and Sidney waited. The eighteenth century passed into the nineteenth. He worked Sundays, holidays, and even during the periods of rest allowed the slaves. He began to fill his drawstring pouch with coins. And his cabin echoed with the happy sounds of two more children born to them—Mahalah and Kitturah—little girls who filled their hearts with joy.

Finally, Levin had several hundred dollars, the sum his master had asked. He approached his owner with the money, and Saunders Griffin, true to his word, gave Levin papers declaring him free.

"Go," he advised his former slave, "there is no such creature as a free black in the South."

Aware of the truth of these words, Levin decided not to tarry. He said good-bye to his wife, kissed his children, and headed for the North.

Although she knew the day would come, Sidney had not anticipated the torment of life without her Levin. Only the love she shared with her children kept her from taking her life.

But in moments of despair, a strong core of strength rose to the surface to sustain her. When days looked dark— before Levin had gotten his free papers—Sidney used to console herself with the hope, "One day, Levin . . . he be free!" Yet now that day had come and gone. As she crumbed her mistress' table or worked at chores in the kitchen, her thoughts were always with Levin far away in the North.

Winter blended into spring on the Griffin place. The white folks in the great house prepared for yet another summer.

"I cain't live without Levin," she finally decided. Shortly afterward she stood in her mother's cabin with her children by her side and ignored the older woman's plea: "Don't go, Sidney!"

"I must!" she cried.

Bidding her mother good-bye, she led the children through the forest of pines.

With the North Star as guide, they quickly walked the leafy path beside the river. They walked all night. With the dawn they found an empty cave for shelter. Night after night they traveled through swamps, forests, and fields. Cold plagued their flesh. Rain pelted them.

When their food dwindled, Sidney foraged for berries. Hunger gnawed their bellies. But never once did she let her courage fade. She trusted God would take them to Levin.

Slowly they advanced northward. With luck on their side, they crossed Mason and Dixon's line separating slave from free soil. By asking about, she was able to contact people who took her to Levin in a place called Greenwich, New Jersey. He could scarcely believe his eyes.

Eager to feed and clothe his family, he took any job he could find—plowing, sowing, or cutting timber in the pine country. He found a one-room cabin in the woods for them while he wandered the countryside in search of work.

One night, with only a sliver of moon above, Sidney waited for Levin to return from work. Feeling uneasy, she paced the floor while her children slept crowded in cots by the log wall. She thought she heard a twig snap outside. Even the sound of the wind through the pines stirred her fanciful mind.

"He be home soon," she told herself.

Just then the door was flung wide, revealing a party of men with ropes and pistols.

"Slave-hunters!" she guessed.

Instinctively, she rushed over to her children in a vain attempt to protect them.

"Grab the wench!" ordered a tall man. Two men grabbed her and tied her wrists behind her back. Then one of them gagged her mouth with a handkerchief. She struggled in vain on the floor where they had thrown her while they tied the children. Then they carried them to a wagon outside.

By the conversation, Sidney could make out the name of the leader, Kincaid, who said he was taking them back to her owner's place in Maryland.

As the wagon rolled along the road leading from town, fear overtook her, fear that she would never see Levin again. They rode a long stretch before the horses stopped at the edge of a town. The driver paid his agents for their part, let them off, then spurred the horses and the wagon raced on through the night.

Finally they reached the owner's place in Maryland where the slave-hunter delivered the fugitives to Mr. Griffin.

Pleased, the planter remarked, "My wandering slaves return."

"Leave Sidney with me!" he ordered. "To the cabins with them!" he waved at the children.

He personally led her to a garret room in his house, saying, "I must cure you of your urge to escape!"

Wisely, she did not resist. As a child she had seen her father's brains blown out by his owner.

Weeks passed. Whenever she finished her chores her owner locked her in the attic. He took her out each morning for chores in the kitchen. He kept this up for several months and would have kept it up indefinitely if Sidney had not decided to try to soften her master's heart. She began to sing the Methodist hymns they both knew so well, hoping he would think her cured.

When he came to fetch her for work she was singing softly. When he brought her back she was humming sweetly.

He began to think: "She seems fair content."

Partly convinced she was cured, he nevertheless continued to lock the door. But in time he relented and decided not to lock her in.

At the first possible moment, Sidney crept quietly down the stairs and out of the house. She went to her children who lived in her mother's cabin. Standing over the cot where her boys, Peter and Levin—aged six and eight—slept, she fought tears and whispered a prayer for God to protect them. Because of the hardships they had faced in their previous flight, she could not take all four. She faced the torment of having to leave her man-children behind, for the frail bodies of the girls would break more readily under the yoke.

She kissed her mother and, clutching the girls, she once again walked out of the slave quarter into the woods with the North Star as guide.

Their flesh ached. Cold and hunger bit them. Soon sickness overtook Kitturah after they had journeyed many miles.

Sidney was forced to leave the child with kind farmers who offered them shelter along the way.

In time, she and Mahalah crossed over Mason and Dixon's line into New Jersey.

Again, she found Levin, who vowed no man would take her from him this time. He took his family to another neighborhood in the pines of Burlington County, New Jersey. They changed their name to Still to evade slave-hunters. For further safety, Sidney changed hers to Charity.

Levin fetched the stricken child. Determined to make a home for them, he hired out wherever he could find work. But when he left his family alone, he urged his wife to use the loaded pistol he had given her.

The sight of the strong black man moving from county to county in search of work became familiar. He plowed and sowed; he reaped the crops. When the earth lay covered with frost he cut timber in the pine country and hauled it to the saw mills in the back of the mule-team wagon. But in spite of his efforts he managed only to eke out a living.

Levin soon found it necessary to hire out the girls to earn their keep. Charity worked beside him in the fields— when she was not milking cows or cleaning pigsties. With the birth of Samuel—on the 26th of February, 1807— Levin vowed to get a decent home for his family at the earliest possible moment.

In order to accomplish this, he accepted work with a man named Mr. Thompson, near Indian Mills, New Jersey. He hoped to advance more rapidly if he worked for only one man.

On the 9th of April, 1812, another son, James, was born. And two years and nine months later, John Nelson joined them.

Levin hired out to a Mr. Cato, nearby, and worked with even greater determination in order to save to buy a piece of land on which he planned to build a cabin. Soon he was able to buy the plot—with the help of his kind employer— in the sparsely inhabited pine country at Shamong, in Burlington County, New Jersey. The one-story house that Levin built from logs he cut himself was completed after months of spare-time work. It boasted two rooms, one of which had a fieldstone hearth on its far wall.

Many children—Mary, Charles, Joseph, and others— were born as the years passed. Some died in childbirth or early childhood. But the children brought joy and laughter to their parents, who worked even harder to make the simple house a place of love.

By the time James was eight, he had already made a reputation for himself as a champion rail splitter, for he had disdained toys and games. Mahalah and Kitturah continued to hire out. And Samuel, the oldest son, worked the land which consisted of several acres now.

Since the family was able to sell what fruit and vegetables it did not consume, Levin had a reserve of cash at the end of the next few years. He invested in more land. Even so, he could not spare the children from chores to attend the village school full time.

Slavery faded rapidly into the past with the upswing of the family's fortunes. But not the torment of the separation Charity had faced when she left her sons behind. She always remembered the pain, which time had never dulled. Although she attempted to hide her anxiety about their plight from Levin, he used to tell her how courageous she had been to make that awesome decision when she kissed them and consigned them to the care of God.

By dint of hard work and frugality, Levin added rich

farmland and orchards. The peach trees grew heavy with fruit, and the pear and apple trees yielded bushel baskets for sale at market. Garden vegetables filled the barn, and the cellar of the house held jars of preserves. They kept pigs and chickens, which provided hearty food for their table.

Another son was born on the 7th of October, 1821. William, resembling his African forefathers from the island of Madagascar, where it was believed Levin's people originated, became the eighteenth child born to Charity Still.

The handsome ebony boy had his chores, as a youth, like all the rest. And like the others, he could not attend school all day, except when it was raining. Until he was seventeen he worked at a variety of jobs—cutting timber and preparing it for market, burning charcoal, and picking cranberries.

He found in James a beloved companion as well as a brother. Both had quick, unusual minds. James wanted to be a doctor while William dreamed of helping his people. The gift for healing and the gift for social service appeared early, but with little opportunity for an education, what could these young men born to a former slave ever hope to do?

William's young mind already had been shaped by the stories about his brothers—Peter and Levin—in slavery even now, and by the tears he saw roll down his mother's cheeks when she thought nobody was around. The good life they lived as blacks free in the North, when he thought of his people in chains, stamped the issue even more indelibly in his heart as a wrong in need of righting. The contrast troubled him. No black man could be free, in his estimation, if all were not. But he was convinced, by what he read, that slavery was destined to last forever.

9

Unable to forget about the slaves, he read everything he could on that as well as many other subjects. One book, in particular, influenced him greatly, *The Young Man's Own Book*. In his free time, he studied English, history, and geography, and worked diligently at learning every subject as thoroughly as he could.

His keen interest in the cause of emancipation led him to subscribe to *The Colored American,* edited by Charles B. Ray and Philip Bell of New York. It was the first anti-slavery newspaper in this country owned and published by black men.

In the fall of 1841, William left the farm. He planned to work in New Jersey until he had saved a little money, and then to go to Philadelphia where greater opportunities and advantages awaited members of his race. Above all he wanted to improve his mind.

The following year, he returned to his family's house because his father died. On Christmas Eve, 1842, he and his sisters and brothers tried to comfort their mother, who sobbed quietly while tears ran down her cheeks. She kept saying, "Levin . . . he be free! Now Levin . . . he be free!"

chapter two

James handled his father's estate. By the time all the bills were paid, the amount left for each of the children came to almost nothing.

James used his share for a still and an old horse. He needed the still to prepare medicines from peppermint, sassafras, and other plants growing wild in the fields. He found a ready market for these preparations among the druggists of Philadelphia. A medical botany book he bought on one of his trips to the city provided knowledge of other medicines and their uses. He studied it constantly and traveled the countryside dispensing his homemade salves, ointments, and cures. He used a cigar box for a medicine chest, placing it in the back of a small horse-drawn wagon with pine-board sides draped in white muslin.

As long as he limited his "medical" practice to the use of salves on external sores and ulcers, he encountered no difficulties. But when on occasion he treated people who were sick with fevers, local physicians scoffed at the "masquerade" of this black man who dared to come among them as a doctor. Soon they ceased all laughter—when people

11

began to call him "Doc" Still and spoke of the strange medicines that cured their ailments.

The doctors threatened to take him into court for practicing without a license. Now James knew he was in trouble! Since he had never graduated from medical school and had no diploma to show, he sought legal counsel in Mount Holly, a town close by. Armed with the knowledge of what he could and could not do, he quietly resumed his work.

"Doc" Still gained a reputation for a remarkable number of cures, mainly of "scrofula" and other skin lesions, including some that had baffled even the learned physicians of the area. In fact, word spread that he had a cure for "skin cancer."

His young wife, Henrietta, and their son James, now occupying an almost bare cabin, began to move into better economic circumstances when James added a small plot of land. Now he had his eye on some land on the corner of the crossroads in Medford Township where one day he hoped to build a lovely home for his family.

Samuel, who lived now with his family in a cabin close to his mother's house, helped with the farm. But William, restless to begin his life's work, left for Philadelphia in the spring of 1844. He found a place to live on Fifth Street above Poplar in a rickety old frame shanty. Short of ready cash and with no immediate prospect of steady work, he faced many hardships that first year away from home.

He accepted a series of odd jobs. Then he found one with the promise of a future in the family of Mrs. E. Langdon Elwyn on West Penn Square. His duties were routine chores about the house and grounds, and since his job didn't consume all his time, he had a chance to read. Mrs. Elwyn encouraged his interest by selecting books from her well-stocked library, hoping to help him stretch his intelligent mind. As she had traveled widely in America as well as in Europe and knew many of the leading public men of the day and their families, she was able to acquaint him with contemporary affairs. She used to talk about her experiences and William listened with great interest.

During this time, William engaged in work at the Sunday school at the Moral Reform Retreat on Lombard Street. He met a fine young woman there, Letitia George, whose interest in her people equaled his. They were married in 1847.

His job with the Elwyns was about to end when he answered an advertisement for combination clerk and handy man at the Anti-slavery office on North Fifth Street. He was hired by a man named James McKim and went to work at the salary of three dollars a week.

Pennsylvania, located as it was, just over Mason and Dixon's line, had since the earliest days been the state, along with New Jersey, where slaves went in fleeing from bondage. Many Quakers, whose religious teachings forced them to see slavery as a moral wrong, lived in or near Philadelphia, and while most did nothing to oppose the laws of the land which approved of the institution, some few devoted their efforts to aiding the fugitive slave when one of the wretched black men was able to cross over the state's border.

Several of these men spoke out earnestly for abolition of slavery. Driven by a strong sense of independence and respect for the right of all men to be free, a group of these like-minded white men banded together to form the Pennsylvania Society for Promoting the Abolition of Slavery. The Society was also interested in improving the lot of the black people already living in Philadelphia. It urged them to enroll their children in the public schools to help dispel the prejudice of a large segment of the population that blacks were inherently of a lower intellectual capacity than whites.

In 1840, the Society formed a committee for the "Improvement of the Colored Race." Its aim was to enlist blacks for work in their own behalf. Another committee made a survey of "Associations among the Colored People of the City for Promoting Scientific and Moral Purposes." The committee hoped to encourage moral reform among blacks where it felt reform was needed, and at the same time it wished to present a more positive image of colored people as a result of its data. Other groups arose which stressed the necessity for good conduct, temperance, and thrift.

In 1817, a Quaker named Thomas Shipley joined the Pennsylvania Abolition Society and took an ardent interest in its activities. In 1833, as a leading member of the society, he met with William Lloyd Garrison, editor of the famous abolitionist newspaper, *The Liberator,* of Boston; Arthur and Lewis Tappan, merchants of Brooklyn, New York; James Birney, a former slaveholder then living in Philadelphia; and many other abolitionists from all over the country at a convention held in Philadelphia. The meeting resulted in the founding of the American Anti-slavery Society. In the same year a number of local societies, such as the Philadelphia Anti-slavery Society, were founded.

A major purpose of the new antislavery societies was to give assistance to the increasing numbers of runaway slaves from the South. Philadelphia was one of the hubs of this work. Men from all walks of life formed the workers in this nucleus. Dr. Bartholemew Fussell cared for the sick slaves. Robert Purvis, mulatto freeborn whose white father brought him and his brother North to educate them, sheltered the fugitives in his home. The Reverend William H. Furness, trained at the Harvard Divinity School, spoke forthrightly from the pulpit of his Unitarian Church against the evils of slavery. Professor Charles Cleveland, who taught at one of the colleges in Philadelphia, tried to remain aloof from the issue of emancipation. He held, like many in the North, an easygoing wish to avoid direct contact with the South on the subject. But the sight of the wretched fugitives forced him to declare himself by organizing the National Liberty Party with the aim of sponsoring a candidate who might run for President. At the same time, the active part which Thomas Shipley took in the new antislavery movement did not diminish his interest in the prosperity and usefulness of the old Pennsylvania Abolition Society. A short time before his death, in 1836, he was elected president of that society.

The Philadelphia Anti-slavery Society printed a newspaper called the Pennsylvania *Freeman*. The newspaper carried an account of antislavery affairs taking place in the state. But with one noticeable exception. Not a word was written about helping runaway slaves. A law which made it a federal crime to aid the fugitive had been enacted by the United States Congress in 1789. Therefore, this area of the work was kept carefully concealed in order not to incriminate any member.

And to further protect the various activities in this area, some of the finest legal talent was made available to the Anti-slavery office by devoted men without whose concerted efforts much of the work to protect the slave would have been doomed to failure.

In 1840, one of the youngest members of the Philadelphia Anti-slavery Society, James McKim, took on the job of Publishing Agent for the committee having jurisdiction over publication of the paper. After the retirement of the former editor he not only published and managed the paper, but was responsible for its editorial content.

This former Presbyterian minister of Scotch-Irish and German background had given up the pulpit when he found a more suitable method to fight against slavery. He was a competent writer and a brilliant strategist. It soon became possible to enlarge his function in the office. With the new role of Corresponding Secretary of the Philadelphia Anti-slavery Society he shared in all antislavery matters—national as well as local.

In this way, the "Underground Railroad," which moved slaves into Canada, came under the partial control and review of this dedicated man in the State of Pennsylvania in the early 1840's.

This aid to fugitive slaves worked like a railroad: "trains," the means of transportation; "conductors," those intrepid souls, white as well as black, who sheltered runaways; "depots," the railroad "stations" where the hunted bondsmen stopped on the way to the free soil of the North to eat and rest; "station-masters," men and women who serviced the stopping-off places; and "stockholders," the friends of the slave who financed the railroad in the name of freedom.

Antislavery societies cropped up in the North. From Ohio to New York. From Indiana to Pennsylvania. From New Jersey to Massachusetts. And in secret places in the South.

As slaves trickled over the southern border of Pennsylvania in ever greater numbers, slave-hunters arose to capture them. These mercenaries, lured in most cases by substantial rewards, defended tenaciously the rights of the owner to his slave.

16

Fearing a mass retrieval, James McKim and other anti-slavery men in Philadelphia, accompanied by legal counsel, sought redress in the courts. At stake lay the future of all colored people, freeborn as well as fugitive slave. For although the country stood half-slave and half-free, the law of Congress provided clearly that a black man, once the "chattel" of his owner, always would remain so.

The following letter came to James McKim:

19th, 4th mo., 1848
Downingtown, Pennsylvania

My Dear Friend:—This morning our family was aroused by the screams of a young colored girl, who has been living with us nearly a year past; but we were awakened only in time to see her borne off by three white men, ruffians indeed, to a carriage at our door, and in an instant she was on her way to the South. I feel so much excited by the attendant circumstances of this daring and atrocious deed, as scarcely to be able to give you a coherent account of it, but I know that it is a duty to make it known, and, I therefore write this immediately.

As soon as the house was opened in the morning, these men who were lurking without, having a carriage in waiting in the street, entered on their horrid errand. They encountered no one in their entrance, except a colored boy, who was making the fire; and who, being frightened at their approach, ran and hid himself; taking a lighted candle from the kitchen, and carrying it up stairs, they went directly to the chamber in which the poor girl lay in a sound sleep. They lifted her from her bed and carried her down stairs. In the entry of the second floor they met one of my sisters, who, hearing an unusual noise, had sprung from her bed. Her screams, and those of the poor girl, who was now thoroughly awakened to

17

the dreadful truth, aroused my father, who hurried undressed from his chamber, on the ground floor. My father's efforts were powerless against the three; they threw him off, and with frightful imprecations hurried the girl to the carriage. Quickly as possible my father started in pursuit, and reached West Chester only to learn that the carriage had driven through the borough at full speed, about half an hour before. They had two horses to their vehicle, and there were three men besides those in the house. These particulars we gather from the colored boy, Ned, who, from his hiding place, was watching them in the road.

Can anything be done for the rescuc of this girl from the kidnappers? We are surprised and alarmed! The deliberate invasion of our house, is a thing unimagined. There must be some informer, who is acquainted with our house and its arrangements, or they never would have come so boldly through. Truly, there is no need to preach about Slavery in the abstract, this individual case combines every wickedness by which human nature can be degraded.

Truly Thy Friend,
Mary B. Thomas

James McKim read her letter with deep regret. Her case proved his point exactly. If the Anti-slavery Society failed to consider and publish facts such as these, it would, indeed, be fighting for a lost cause.

Therefore, when he received in the mail, a short time later, the following excerpt from her, he read it with great interest:

As to detail, the whole transaction was like a flash to those who saw the miserable ending. I was impelled to write without delay, by the thought that it would be in time for the "Freeman," and that any procrastination on my part might jeopard others of these suffering people, who are living, as was this poor girl, in fancied security. Our consternation was inexpressible; our sorrow and indignation deepen daily, as the thought returns of the awful announcement with which we were awakened: they have carried Martha to the South. To do what will be of most service to the cause—not to their cause—ours—that of our race, is our burning desire.

Little by little, the antislavery men in Philadelphia prepared themselves to do battle. The illegal act of helping runaway slaves began to lose its lawless aspect with the arrival in that city of an increasing number of fugitive slaves.

Word came through, via the Underground Railroad, that a couple would arrive at the Anti-slavery office in Philadelphia. Mr. McKim asked his young clerk and confidant, William Still, to accompany him for their arrival.

Eager to involve himself directly in antislavery work, young Still witnessed the arrival of the fugitives from Georgia and recorded their amazing escape. This became the first of such records he would keep for the history of that mysterious "road."

William and Ellen Craft, husband and wife, devised and carried out a successful escape from their masters who owned a plantation in the deep South. In order to accomplish this feat, they pretended to be a traveling slave master and slave. Ellen, fair enough to pass for a white person, acted the part of slave master. She had her hair cut in the style worn by rich young planters and dressed in male attire; and her husband, William, dark-skinned, played the part of her manservant.

Being beardless presented problems. Therefore, she muffled her face to conceal "a swelling due to the tooth- ache." Since it was the custom for slave masters traveling overnight to sign the registries of the hotels, she had her right arm tied in a sling. With a cane in her other hand, and wearing glasses tinted with green over her weak eyes— and hard of hearing, as well—she needed her servant close to her at all times.

William was perfect in the role. He was smart, and active, and very attentive to all of his master's wishes.

On and on they moved northward. When they came to Charleston, the planter was treated with the utmost chivalry. Then they arrived in Richmond, with similar results. But Baltimore was the test.

At the depot in that city, the servant was asked for tickets for his master and himself.

"Of course, your master can have tickets," said the ticket agent, "but bonds will have to be entered before you can get a ticket."

Before William could reply, the agent added, "It is a rule of this office to require bonds for all Negroes applying for tickets to go north, and none but gentlemen of well-known responsibility will be taken."

"I know nothing about that," replied William, with bravado. "I am simply traveling with my young master to take care of him. Indeed, his health is in such a delicate state that I fear he may not be able to hold out in order to reach Philadelphia where he hastens for medical treatment." Trembling visibly, the slave added, "My master must not be detained."

Feeling sorry for him, the ticket master waived the old rule and furnished the tickets. The Crafts boarded the cars and departed in Philadelphia when the train arrived. They found their way to the Anti-slavery office, where in the presence of officials they removed their disguises and related the story of their escape.

After a few days of rest at William Still's home, the valiant lady began to forget the ordeal which she had survived in the last weeks. No longer attired in a fine black suit and boots proper to a slave master, she looked every inch a lady, while her husband, a man of marked and natural abilities, stood by her side willing and able to protect her.

But the increase in slave-capturing incidents in Philadelphia forced the members of the Anti-slavery Society to consider a permanent residence for the pair. The consensus pointed to Boston, Massachusetts, headquarters of the abolition movement in America. Since it had been about a generation since a fugitive had been recaptured and taken to the South from that state, it was conceded that another such incident would not be tolerated in the Bay State.

The pair went to Boston, where they were met by anti-slavery people. So sure was everyone that the North was safe from slave-catchers now, they published the news of their arrival in the newspapers with no reservations.

Before the former slaves settled down, they requested, as new citizens of Massachusetts, the privilege of a marriage ceremony in that state which they believed more appropriate to the mores of the civilized world than that permitted them in the South. Through friends, they met Theodore Parker, a Unitarian minister who agreed to unite them in matrimony according to the laws of a free state.

He performed the ceremony—this fearless and renowned advocate of equal rights—and after the rites, presented to William Craft a revolver and dirk-knife which he counseled him to use in the manful defense of his wife and himself.

Shortly after this episode, a reinforcement of the earlier fugitive slave law was enacted by the Congress of the United States. In 1850, a law appeared with teeth in it, "An act respecting fugitives from justice, and persons escaping from the service of their masters." Fines and time in the penitentiary were the penalties levied against those who aided the runaway slave, wherever he fled.

It began to dawn on the ardent antislavery men of the day that the law stood on the side of the slave owners and if they hoped to oppose it in the courts, the fight would be an uphill battle. Facing staggering odds, they had one choice now—dig in and fight. To win they had to seize the opportunity each moment presented.

More and more of James McKim's time was devoted to the slave cases appearing before the courts. And in consequence of this, he left a great number of clerical chores connected with the office in the care of his trusted clerk and confidant, William Still.

Young Still spent long hours becoming acquainted with the way the Anti-slavery office was run. His duties included reading several Southern newspapers which ran ads of runaway slaves. This information gave him notice of whom to expect at the office in time to come. He acquainted himself with abolitionists who wrote about slaves they helped to escape and who would pass through Philadelphia. He distributed handbills announcing the presence in the city of notorious slave-catchers.

One evening, on the 1st of August, 1850, the black man sat at his desk when he was interrupted by a knock at his door.

"Come in!" he shouted.

He heard another knock.

"The door is open!" he shouted. "Come in!"

Still recognized the elderly visitor who stood there; but he did not know the middle-aged black man who stood beside him.

"Mr. Still," the old man said, "I am sorry to disturb you,

but this gentleman, Mr. Gist, seeks his people. Since I was unable to locate them, I brought him to see you."

Looking up from his work on the desk, William scrutinized the man who stood before him. About forty-five years old, his face was lined with deep furrows and his threadbare clothes hung on his stooped frame. His body, powerful still, appeared as though weighted with the cares of long years of slavery. And in his calloused hands he carried a faded carpet bag.

"Sit down, Mr. Gist," the clerk said, showing him to a chair by the desk.

The visitor accepted, sitting tensely on the edge of it.

"Reverend Byas," William spoke to the minister, "did not anyone at the church know of his people?"

"No, William, not even the older members."

Turning to the anxious stranger, the clerk asked, "Mr. Gist, tell me your story. Perhaps I can help you."

"I come for Momma and my sister 'Merica."

"How long have you been separated?"

"Mos' forty yar."

William Still listened to the story which the man related. He told how he had received his free papers in Bainbridge, Alabama, where he had served a man by the name of Gist. He told of his journey to Philadelphia to find his people. But when he spoke of his brother, named Levin, who had died on the plantation, William Still could scarcely believe his ears.

Afraid to unleash his emotions, the young clerk stared into the frightened eyes of the former slave. Gaining his presence of mind, he turned to Reverend Byas and said, "The hour is growing late, Sir. Would you mind very much if I ask Mr. Gist some questions? I promise to see that he gets to the rooming house."

23

"Not at all, William," the elderly gentleman replied. With that he turned and left the two men in the room of the Anti-slavery office to talk.

For a few moments, William faced the man in silence. He scanned every feature of his face, the broad nose and the heavy lips. He stared into the man's eyes which were stamped indelibly with the suffering of many years.

Then he reached over and touched the stranger's hands.

Gist cringed. His master's warnings through the years to beware the abolitionists frightened him. And black abolitionists, most of all. Therefore, the freedman rose from his chair and moved quickly toward the door.

"Don't run away, Peter," William said softly.

Reluctantly, Peter returned to his chair.

"What would you say if I said I was your brother?" asked the clerk.

Again, Peter stood up.

"There is no doubt in my mind. You, and Levin who died, are my brothers our mother has wept for these many years."

Trembling, Peter asked, "What of 'Merica?"

"Our sister's name is Mahalah. But how could you remember her name for more than forty years?"

The brothers hugged each other while each fought tears. Confused, yet overjoyed, the pair remained in the office room for a long while before William took his newly found brother to a carriage and the ride back to his room.

"I'll tell our sister, Mary, who lives here in Philadelphia, in the morning. She'll be delighted. I will post a letter to James so he'll expect us."

"Father, he gone?" asked Peter.

"These last years," replied William.

When he returned to their rooms, William told the news to his wife, Letitia.

"Can you be very sure?" she asked.

"I have no doubt whatsoever," he replied. "He is the image of mother and James."

William posted a letter to James in Medford, New Jersey, that very night.

Later, when a reply was received, William and Mary took their brother Peter to the ferry which crossed the Delaware River to the opposite side, at Long Branch, New Jersey. There they boarded the stage for Medford—twenty or thirty miles out in the country.

They met James at his house where he and his wife, Henrietta, made them comfortable for the night before the trip to their mother's house the following morning. James welcomed his brother Peter warmly. And Peter marveled at the comfort his brother James enjoyed compared to the wretched life he had endured as a slave.

In the morning, the party went to their mother's house, some eight or ten miles farther out in the country.

When they arrived, the aging woman at first failed to recognize the stranger her sons brought with them.

Although the plan had been for him to break the news of his identity to her gently—to spare her—Peter could not restrain himself.

"Momma!" he shouted, moving close to her. "It be me— Peter!"

Her eyes, clouded with age, stared into his. Then tears rolled down her cheeks. She stretched her arms to receive her son.

"Peter, son?" she whispered.

He kissed her and wept.

"An' what of Levin?" she asked.

"He be free," replied the freed bondsman. "Levin . . . he be free!"

Sadness swept her face. She remained silent a moment. Then she said, "Thank God almighty!"

James and William helped her to a chair beside the hearth. She relived that terrible day when she decided to leave the boys in order to insure her safe flight to Levin. The years had not lessened the torment she endured.

But now her prayers had been answered.

Throughout the afternoon, they talked of the events which filled the years of the long separation. And Peter told of how he had lived as a slave. But then he spoke of his wife, Vina, who waited on the plantation with their children, Catherine, Peter, and Levin.

"What would you do if you could not be reunited with your family?" William asked.

"I'd as soon go out of this world."

Haunted by the long history of oppression visited upon members of their family, the Stills sat and listened to the tale of Peter's suffering.

He began with the years after the flight of their mother from Maryland. Saunders Griffin, their owner, sold them at auction to a man named John Fisher who lived in Lexington, Kentucky. He took his young slaves to work there in his brickyards where he had interest in a masonry business as well as a plantation a mile or so out of town.

He put Levin, the older boy, to work in the brickyard and sent Peter to herd the cows with an older slave. His lands spread out to the Henry Clay place in Ashland, bringing Peter into contact with the Clay children, Theodore and Thomas. Although it was not the custom for white boys to romp with slaves, a friendship developed which Mrs. Clay smiled on benignly.

In fact, she used to listen to the story Peter told of the separation from his mother and sisters who went up north by the Delaware River. Moved by his sadness, she tried to console him. The kind white woman sent mugs of cool milk and delicious cakes for the children to eat when they lingered in the fields with her boys.

With their childhood fading fast behind them, the boys faced a new and harsher life. When Peter was thirteen, they were sold to a master named Nat Gist, of Lexington, Kentucky. He paid four hundred and fifty dollars each for them.

In 1817, Nat Gist died. Levi, one of his kinfolk, settled his affairs. He sent half of the slaves—six—to Bainbridge, Alabama, to work on another relative's plantation. Levin went south to William Gist's, and Peter remained in Ashland, where Levi hired him out to a man named Young.

Peter continued to enjoy his friendship with the Clays. But when Young did not need him the following year, he too was sent to the Gists in Alabama.

Three years later, Levi, who now owned Peter, built a magnificent house in Bainbridge, and used Peter, then twenty-one, for his house servant.

But Levin continued in the fields. Always in poor health, he managed to bear the joyless days because of the love he had for a slave girl named Fanny—from the neighboring plantation. When his attachment for her became very deep, he asked her owner for permission to marry her. Reluctantly, her owner gave him permission; but only with the stipulation that the young slave husband abide by the rules he set for visits, which would be limited.

For a short time, Levin enjoyed happy moments when he was permitted to see his wife. Then his health, always frail, grew worse. Unable to do his former quota of work, he felt the sting of the rawhide lash on his back. But when it became known to the master that he had been seen visiting his wife without permission, the irate master ordered young Levin whipped a total of three hundred and seventeen times.

From then on, Levin grew weaker. The sight of his broken slave softened the heart of the planter. He relented, allowing the slave to be with his wife more often. But not long after the severe lashing, Levin died.

Peter, with help from another slave, buried Levin under Alabama soil. Peter knelt beside the mound of earth with a heap of stones to mark the grave, and said a prayer for his brother's soul. And fearing he himself would die of sorrow, Peter raised his eyes upward to heaven and vowed he would be free. Not like Levin, in death; but really free—someday.

When Levi Gist died Peter was sold to Jimmy Hogun of Tuscumbia, Alabama. He pleaded with Hogun and his wife for his freedom but was refused again and again. He even feigned a chronic cough, hoping they would change their minds because of his supposedly poor health. But they did not.

Finally, in 1849, Jimmy Hogun died and one of his relatives placed the slaves up for sale. Joseph Friedman, a moneylender in the town, became Peter's owner, and he promised to give him his freedom for five hundred dollars. Peter gave his new master all the money he had saved, three hundred dollars. Their understanding was that as soon as Peter gave him the remaining two hundred, Friedman would issue him free papers.

28

Aware that the law did not permit a slave to buy his freedom, Friedman intended to take Peter out of the South as soon as it was possible. When they arrived in the North he would let him go free.

By September, 1849, Peter had saved one hundred dollars which he promptly handed to his master. In March, 1850, he paid him another sixty dollars. And in April, he paid forty.

As he had promised, his new master wrote a paper listing the several payments made by Peter. He headed it with the words: "Certificate of Freedom."

It read as follows:

Rec'd Tuscumbia, Alabama, January 26th, 1849, of my boy, Peter—
three hundred dollars $300.00

Joseph Friedman

Rec'd September 1st, 1849—
eighty-eight dollars and
      twelve dollars

Rec'd March 29th,
      1850, of Peter $60.00

Joseph Friedman

$460.00

Rec'd April 16th,
      1850 $40.00

$500.00

For, and in consideration of the above $500.00, I have this 16th day of April, 1850, given Peter a Bill of Sale, and given him his freedom.

Joseph Friedman
Tuscumbia, Alabama
April 16, 1850

White-haired now, Peter dreamed of finding his mother and father who lived by the Delaware River with his sisters. But the pain of leaving his beloved wife and children behind in slavery disturbed the joy he at last had earned. When his nominal master urged him to prepare for a journey north with him, Peter swore to his wife and family he would come for them after he had found his people.

After Peter had earned eighty dollars from over-work to defray his expenses north, he kissed his wife and children good-bye and left with Joseph Friedman's brother, Isaac, who was bound for Ohio on business. They took the boat to Cincinnati, where Isaac left him, warning him to stay on board until the boat had reached Pittsburgh. Peter thanked him for everything. Then the boat moved on. For the first time since leaving the plantation, he trembled for fear he might be mistaken for a fugitive slave.

At Pittsburgh he went ashore and took a stage for Philadelphia, traveling through the Allegheny Mountains. He arrived in Philadelphia on August 1st. A stranger in Pittsburgh had given him the name of a boardinghouse in the black community and told him to go to churches if he needed help in finding his people. At one of these churches, he met Reverend Byas, who, unable to help him, brought him to the Anti-slavery office on North Fifth Street.

Like Aeneas, fate had driven Peter there.

Engravings and Photographs

An invoice of ten negroes sent this day to John
B Williamson by Geo Kremer named & cost as fol—
lows

. To wit .. Betsey Kackley . . . . . . $.410. 00
Nancy Aulick 515. 00
Harry & Helen Miller . . .1200. 00
Mary Kootz 600. 00
Betsey Ott? . . . . . . , 560. 00
Isaac & Fanny Brent . . 992. 00
Lucinda Luckett 467. 50
George Smith 510. 00
Amount of my traveling expences & boarding 254. 50
of lot No 9 not included in the other bills .. 39. 50
Kremers expences. Transporting lot N 9 to Rich.d 51 . . 00
Carryall hire .. 6. 00
$ 5351. 00

I have this day delivered the above named negroes
costing includeing my expences and other expences
five thousand three hundred & fifty dollars this May
26th 1835 —
                              John. W. Pittman
I did intend to leave Nancy child but she made
such a damned fuss I had to let her take it I could
of got fifty Dollars for so you must add forty Dollars
to the above

The commercial value of ten Negro slaves
is itemized in this invoice dated 1835.

James McKim

Peter Still

Charity Still

William Craft

Ellen Craft

Jane Johnson

Passmore Williamson

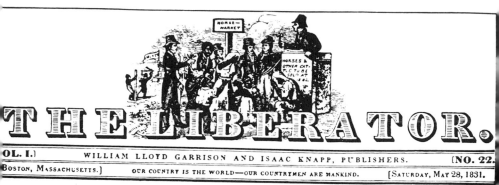

THE LIBERATOR.

VOL. I.]   WILLIAM LLOYD GARRISON AND ISAAC KNAPP, PUBLISHERS.   [NO. 22.

BOSTON, MASSACHUSETTS.]   OUR COUNTRY IS THE WORLD—OUR COUNTRYMEN ARE MANKIND.   [SATURDAY, MAY 28, 1831.

The Granger Collection

The Liberator, the most influential antislavery newspaper of the time, began publication in 1831 and continued until 1865.

The Granger Collection

William Lloyd Garrison, founder of *The Liberator.*

chapter three

William Still reluctantly turned his attention at the Anti-slavery office from his brother's plight to an article appearing in Garrison's *Liberator,* dated November 1, 1850. He read:

SLAVE HUNTERS IN BOSTON
Our city, for a week past, has been thrown into a state of intense excitement by the appearance of two prowling villains, named Hughes and Knight, from Macon, Georgia, for the purpose of seizing William and Ellen Craft, under the infernal Fugitive Slave Bill, and carrying them back to the hell of slavery. Since the days of '76, there has not been such a popular demonstration on the side of human freedom in this region. The humane and patriotic contagion has infected all classes. Scarcely any other subject has been talked about in the streets, or in the social circle. . . .

The article pointed out that a judge had issued a warrant for the arrest of the Crafts, but antislavery sentiment in general, and hatred of the Fugitive Slave Law, in particular, ran so high no one could immediately be found to serve it. Instead, antislavery lawyers in Boston arranged to have Hughes and Knight arrested on a charge of slander against the Crafts. They were bailed out and then arrested again on a charge of conspiracy to kidnap and abduct William Craft. The newspaper printed a letter Knight had written to William Craft, in a vain effort to entice him to a Boston hotel.

Mrs. George Hilliard broke the news to Ellen that slavehunters sought to return her to slavery. This Bostonian, who lived on Beacon Hill, expressed her sentiments in a letter to a friend:

In regard to William and Ellen Craft, it is true that we received her at our house when the first warrant under the act of eighteen hundred and fifty was issued.

Dr. Bowditch called upon us to say, that the warrant must be for William and Ellen, as they were the only fugitives here known to have come from Georgia, and the Dr. asked what we could do. I went to the house of the Rev. F. T. Gray, on Mt. Vernon street, where Ellen was working with Miss Dean, an upholsteress, a friend of ours, who told us she would teach Ellen her trade. I proposed to Ellen to come and do some work for me, intending not to alarm her. My manner, which I supposed to be indifferent and calm, *betrayed* me, and she threw herself into my arms, sobbing and weeping. She, however, recovered her composure as soon as we reached the street, and was *very firm* ever after.

My husband wished her, by all means, to be brought to our house, and to remain under his protection, saying: "I am perfectly willing to meet the penalty, should she be found here, but I will never give her up." The penalty, you remember, was six months' imprisonment and a thousand dollars fine. William Craft went, after a time, to Lewis Hayden. He was at first, as Dr. Bowditch told us, "barricaded in his shop on Cambridge street." I saw him there, and he said, "Ellen must not be left at your house." "Why? William," said I,

44

"do you think we would give her up?" "Never," said he, "but Mr. Hilliard is not only our friend, but he is a U.S. Commissioner, and should Ellen be found in his house, he must resign his office, as well as incur the penalty of the law, and I will not subject a friend to such a punishment for the sake of our safety." Was not this noble, when you think how small was the penalty that any one could receive for aiding slaves to escape, compared to the fate which threatened them in case they were captured? William C. made the same objection to having his wife taken to Mr. Ellis Gray Loring's, he also being a friend and a Commissioner.

The slave-hunters left in dismay. After the storm of excitement had subsided partially, their friends decided that the Crafts would not be safe anywhere in America. By means of generous donations, the fare was collected to enable the pair to sail for the safety of England.

Dismayed by the recent attempt of slave-hunters to penetrate as far north as Boston, the antislavery world awaited the next assault upon its bastions. Not in the recent past had the abolitionists been threatened like this. Therefore, in order to protect themselves, they dug in and prepared a defense against similar proslavery attacks.

The abolition cause, hitherto fairly unpopular, received letters of praise for its efforts. Those citizens who sat on the fence regarding the slavery issue came forth in favor of Garrison's sentiments. For the first time, the lonely, outspoken advocate of emancipation had reason to believe the people were beginning to think about the issues which slavery had introduced.

In Philadelphia, James McKim printed in the Pennsylvania *Freeman* the story of Peter Still's life, called "The Kidnapped and the Ransomed." Except for the fact that his mother was a fugitive slave—known only by the Quaker, Benjamin Lundy, a devoted friend of the slave and early antislavery man—the whole wretched tale of the black man's suffering lay before the antislavery world.

The article caught the attention of a white man named Seth Concklin. Being of a sympathetic and humane nature, as well as a man insensible to fear, he volunteered to go into the South to rescue Peter's wife and children.

When the offer came to James McKim and William Still, they decided not to confide in the other members of the Anti-slavery Society, not only because the scheme appeared to present great danger to the good Samaritan, but also because the matter of Peter Still and his family's dilemma was a personal one in regard to the clerk. Then too, on first reflection, the idea of such an undertaking struck them as perfectly appalling. Not only did they acquaint Concklin with all the dangers and difficulties he would encounter through hundreds of miles of slave territory, but they pointed out that the journey might cost him his life.

The determination displayed by Concklin did not flag at a recital of the dangers. William Still marveled at the bravery the stranger showed at that meeting, but was able to convince him to give the matter more thought before deciding on the journey. Then he presented Peter with the white man's plan.

The problem of buying his loved ones under the laws of Alamaba, which denied the right of a slave to buy himself, much less his wife and children, faced them like an insurmountable obstacle. Yet Peter had stayed away from his loved ones as long as he could.

He took his carpet bag in his hand, and began the sixteen-hundred-mile journey to the plantation. Before he left, he informed his brother he would return with some personal article of clothing from his wife which he would present to Concklin. Then, if the white man was still determined to make the trip, he could bring it back to Vina, who would recognize him as a friend.

Taking several hundred dollars with him to pay his way on the steamer and to cover other expenses, Peter went south. His plan was not to appeal to his family's owner for their freedom, because he thought it best not to raise the wrath of the slave master. The law and public opinion being deadly opposed to the awakening of the spirit of freedom in slaves in the deep South, he was forced to consider other means.

His approach was very quiet. Peter did not mention to a soul, except his own family, his former master, Friedman, and one other friend, a slave, a word about where he had been, the offer he had received, or anything about his intentions. Instead, he confided to his wife the generous offer made by the kind man named Concklin who would come for her and their children. And he told her what he had learned from his brother about the Underground Railroad. Although they had never tasted freedom a single hour in their lives, they hated slavery.

Parting tearfully, the couple pledged to follow a plan that consisted of Peter's taking Vina's cape with him to give to the white man who would come for her. When she saw it again she was to trust the man who held it.

Peter returned to Philadelphia where he had an interview with Concklin. He gave him a full description of the country and of his family. He told him that he had discussed the matter of the rescue in detail with his family. And he gave him the cape and several other small articles to take back with him.

Seth declined to say good-bye to his two sisters who lived

in Philadelphia because their close relationship might have made his parting too tearful. With his mind made up, nothing remained now but for him to leave the city. He took two or three small articles of clothing with him in a carpet sack and the sum of one hundred dollars to defray his expenses for a time. His plan was to meet the family, get acquainted, and to prepare them to join him at the wharf, where he would boldly assume the role of slave master and the family, naturally, that of slaves. In this way he hoped to reach Cincinnati directly before their owner had discovered their escape. There Levi Coffin, Underground Railroad stationmaster, was instructed to aid him.

But due to Southern irregularity—two or three days' delay, affecting the day scheduled for departure, was not unusual with steamers—this plan was abandoned. What this heroic man endured from a series of severe struggles and unyielding exertions while he traveled thousands of miles on water and on foot—hungry and fatigued   rowing his living freight for seven days and seven nights in a skiff, is told in the following letters he wrote to William Still:

Eastport, Miss., Feb. 3, 1851

To Wm. Still:—Our friends in Cincinnati have failed finding anybody to assist me on my return [North]. Searching the country opposite Paducah, I find that the whole country fifty miles round is inhabited only by Christian wolves. It is customary, when a strange negro is seen, for any white man to seize the negro and convey such negro through and out of the State of Illinois to Paducah, K., and lodge such stranger in Paducah jail, and there claim such reward as may be offered by the master.

There is no regularity by the steamboats on the Tennessee river. I was four days getting to Florence from Paducah.

48

Sometimes they are four days starting, from the time appointed, which alone puts to rest the plan for returning by steamboat. The distance from the mouth of the river to Florence, is from between three hundred and five to three hundred and forty-five miles by the river; by land, two hundred and fifty, or more.

I arrived at the shoe shop on the plantation, one o'clock, Tuesday, 28th. William and two boys were making shoes. I immediately gave the first signal, anxiously waiting thirty minutes for an opportunity to give the second and main signal, during which time I was very sociable. It was rainy and muddy—my pants were rolled up to the knees. I was in the character of a man seeking employment in this country. End of thirty minutes gave the second signal.

William appeared unmoved; soon sent out the boys; instantly sociable; Peter and Levin at the Island; one of the young masters with them; not safe to undertake to see them till Saturday night, when they would be at home; appointed a place to see Vina in an open field, that night; they to bring me something to eat; our interview only four minutes; I left; appeared by night; dark and cloudy; at ten o'clock appeared William; exchanged signals; led me a few rods to where stood Vina; gave her the signal sent by Peter; our interview ten minutes; she did not call me "master," nor did she say "sir," by which I knew she had confidence in me.

Our situation being dangerous, we decided that I meet Peter and Levin on the bank of the river early dawn of day, Sunday, to establish the laws. During our interview, William prostrated on his knees, and face to the ground; arms sprawling; head cocked back, watching for wolves, by which position a man can see better in the dark. No house to go to safely, traveled round till morning, eating hoe cake which William had given me for supper; next day going around to get employment. I thought of William, who is a Christian preacher, and of the Christian preachers in Pennsylvania.

49

One watching for wolves by night, to rescue Vina and her three children from Christian licentiousness; the other standing erect in open day, seeking the praise of men.

During the four days waiting for the important Sunday morning, I thoroughly surveyed the rocks and shoals of the river from Florence seven miles up, where will be my place of departure. General notice was taken of me as being a stranger, lurking around. Fortunately, there are several small grist mills within ten miles around. No taverns here, as in the North; any planter's house entertains travelers occasionally.

One night I stayed at a medical gentleman's, who is not a large planter; another night at an ex-magistrate's house in South Florence—a Virginian by birth—one of the late census takers; told me that many more persons cannot read and write than is reported; one fact, amongst many others, that many persons who do not know the letters of the alphabet, have learned to write their own names; such are generally reported readers and writers.

It being customary for a stranger not to leave the house early in the morning where he has lodged, I was under the necessity of staying out all night Saturday, to be able to meet Peter and Levin, which was accomplished in due time. When we approached, I gave my signal first; immediately they gave theirs. I talked freely. Levin's voice, at first, evidently trembled. No wonder, for my presence universally attracted attention by the lords of the land. Our interview was less than one hour; the laws were written. I to go to Cincinnati to get a rowing boat and provisions; a first class clipper boat to go with speed. To depart from the place where the laws were written, on Saturday night of the first of March. I to meet one of them at the same place Thursday night previous to the fourth Saturday from the night previous to the Sunday when the laws were written. We to go down the Tennessee river to some place up the Ohio, not yet decided on, in our row boat. Peter and Levin are good oarsmen. So am I. Telegraph station at Tuscumbia, twelve miles from the plantation, also at Paducah.

Came from Florence to here Sunday night by steamboat. Eastport is in Mississippi. Waiting here for a steamboat to go down; paying one dollar a day for board. Like other taverns here, the wretchedness is indescribable; no pen, ink, paper or newspaper to be had; only one room for everybody, excepting the gambling rooms. It is difficult for me to write. Vina intends to get a pass for Catherine and herself for the first Sunday in March.

The bank of the river where I met Peter and Levin is two miles from the plantation. I have avoided saying I am from Philadelphia. Also avoided talking about negroes. I never talked so much about milling before. I consider most of the trouble over, till I arrive in a free state with my crew, the first week in March; then I will have to be wiser than Christian serpents, and more cautious than doves. I do not consider it safe to keep this letter in my possession, yet I dare not put it in the post-office here; there is so little business in these post-offices that notice might be taken.

I am evidently watched; everybody knows me to be a miller. I may write again when I get to Cincinnati, if I should have time. The ex-magistrate, with whom I stayed in South Florence, held three hours' talk with me, exclusive of our morning talk. Is a man of good general information; he was exceedingly inquisitive. "I am from Cincinnati, formerly from the *State of New York*." I had no opportunity to get anything to eat from seven o'clock Tuesday morning till six o'clock Wednesday evening, except the hoe cake, and no sleep.

Florence is the head of navigation for small steamboats. Seven miles, all the way up to my place of departure, is swift water, and rocky. Eight hundred miles to Cincinnati. I found all things here as Peter told me, except the distance of the river. South Florence contains twenty white families, three warehouses of considerable business, a post-office, but no school. McKiernon is here waiting for a steamboat to go to New Orleans, so we are in company.

A fortnight later, William Still received the second letter from Seth Concklin.

Princeton, Gibson County, Indiana, Feb. 18, 1851

To Wm. Still:—The plan is to go to Canada, on the Wabash, opposite Detroit. There are four routes to Canada. One through Illinois, commencing above and below Alton; one through to North Indiana, and the Cincinnati route, being the largest route in the United States.

I intended to have gone through Pennsylvania, but the risk going up the Ohio river has caused me to go to Canada. Steamboat traveling is universally condemned; though many go in boats, consequently many get lost. Going in a skiff is new, and is approved of in my case. After I arrive at the mouth of the Tennessee river, I will go up the Ohio seventy-five miles, to the mouth of the Wabash, then up the Wabash, forty-four miles to New Harmony, where I shall go ashore by night, and go thirteen miles east, to Charles Grier, a farmer, (colored man), who will entertain us, and the next night convey us sixteen miles to David Stormon, near Princeton, who will take the command, and I be released.

David Stormon estimates the expenses from his house to Canada, at forty dollars, without which, no sure protection will be given. They might be instructed concerning the course, and beg their way through without money. If you wish to do what should be done, you will send me fifty dollars, in a letter, to Princeton, Gibson county, Ind., so as to arrive there by the 8th of March. Eight days should be estimated for a letter to arrive from Philadelphia.

The money to be State Bank of Ohio, or State Bank, or Northern Bank of Kentucky, or any other Eastern bank. Send no notes larger than twenty dollars.

Levi Coffin had no money for me. I paid twenty dollars for the skiff. No money to get back to Philadelphia. It was not understood that I would have to be at any expense seeking aid.

One half of my time has been used trying to find persons to assist, when I may arrive on the Ohio river, in which I have failed, except Stormon.

Having no letter of introduction to Stormon from any source, on which I could fully rely, I traveled two hundred miles around, to find out his stability. I have found many Abolitionists, nearly all who have made propositions, which themselves would not comply with, and nobody else would. Already I have traveled over three thousand miles. Two thousand and four hundred by steamboat, two hundred by railroad, one hundred by stage, four hundred on foot, forty-eight in a skiff.

I have yet five hundred miles to go to the plantation, to commence operations. I have been two weeks on the decks of steamboats, three nights out, two of which I got perfectly wet. If I had had paper money, as McKim desired, it would have been destroyed. I have not been entertained gratis at any place except Stormon's. I had one hundred and twenty-six dollars when I left Philadelphia, one hundred from you, twenty-six mine.

Telegraphed to station at Evansville, thirty-three miles from Stormon's, and at Vinclure's, twenty-five miles from Stormon's. The Wabash route is considered the safest route. No one has ever been lost from Stormon's to Canada. Some have been lost between Stormon's and the Ohio. The wolves have never suspected Stormon. Your asking aid in money for a case properly belonging east of Ohio, is detested. If

53

you have sent money to Cincinnati, you should recall it. I will have no opportunity to use it.

Seth Concklin, Princeton, Gibson county, Ind.

P.S. First of April, will be about the time Peter's family will arrive opposite Detroit. You should inform yourself how to find them there. I may have no opportunity.

I will look promptly for your letter at Princeton, till the 10th of March, and longer if there should have been any delay by the mails.

Concklin arrived in Indiana, in March, at the designated place, with Peter's wife and children. He wrote a letter to William Still portraying in the most thrilling terms his flight from Alabama and his arrival in Indiana. He stated that, owing to some unforeseen delay on the part of the family, instead of leaving early in the morning, they did not reach the designated place till near daybreak, which greatly exposed them in passing a certain town which he had hoped to avoid.

Intent only in completing the journey without further delay, he decided to start, at all costs, ignoring the dangers of passing the town in daylight. For safety's sake he ordered the passengers to lie flat on the bottom of the skiff, and covered them with blankets to conceal them from the bright rays of the early morning sun, or rather from the "Christian wolves" who might spy them from the shore.

The wind gusted. Concklin rowed heroically. But he was hailed from the shore by loud shouts. Now he faced his greatest crisis. Ignoring them, he rowed on. Then one or two guns were fired in the direction of the boat; but he continued to ignore the warning. He hoped that the wild sound of the winds might convince those who fired that he had not heard.

The last letter Still ever received from Concklin told of this terrible ordeal. But it was filled with the happy news that soon he would deliver the slaves to Philadelphia as he had promised. Peter cried for joy as he prepared to greet them.

In those few days all doubts disappeared, and the hope was cherished that his wife and children would meet him on the Canadian side of the border as planned. But, unfortunately, before the few days had passed, a brief news item appeared in an edition of the Philadelphia *Ledger*.

Runaway Negroes Caught.—At Vincennes, Indiana, on Saturday last, a white man and four negroes were arrested. The negroes belong to B. McKiernon, of South Florence, Alabama, and the man who was running them off calls himself John H. Miller. The prisoners were taken charge of by the Marshall of Evansville.

April 9th.

The joy of Peter and his relatives turned to gloom when they received these sad tidings. Shortly afterward William Still received a letter from a faithful antislavery man named N. R. Johnston, who described the arrival of Concklin and the fugitives in Indiana and their subsequent capture.

Evansville, Indiana, March 31st, 1851

Wm. Still: *Dear Sir,*—On last Tuesday I mailed a letter to you, written by Seth Concklin. I presume you have received that letter. It gave an account of his rescue of the family of your brother. If that is the last news you have had from them, I have very painful intelligence for you. They passed on from near Princeton, where I saw them and had a lengthy interview with them, up north, I think twenty-three miles above Vincennes, Ind., where they were seized by a

55

party of men, and lodged in jail. Telegraphic dispatches were sent all through the South. I have since learned that the Marshall of Evansville received a dispatch from Tuscumbia, to look out for them. By some means, he and the master, so says report, went to Vincennes and claimed the fugitives, chained Mr. Concklin, and hurried all off. Mr. Concklin wrote to Mr. David Stormon, Princeton, as soon as he was cast into prison, to find bail. So soon as we got the letter and could get off, two of us were about setting off to render all possible aid, when we were told they all had passed, a few hours before, through Princeton, Mr. Concklin in chains. What kind of process was had, if any, I know not. I immediately came down to this place, and learned that they had been put on a boat at 3 P.M. I did not arrive till 6. Now all hopes of their recovery are gone. No case so enlisted my sympathies. I had seen Mr. Concklin in Cincinnati. I had given him aid and counsel. I happened to see them after they landed in Indiana. I heard Peter and Levin tell their tale of suffering, shed tears of sorrow for them all; but now, since they have fallen a prey to the unmerciful blood-hounds of this state, and have again been dragged back to unrelenting bondage, I am entirely unmanned. And poor Concklin! I fear for him. When he is dragged back to Alabama, I fear they will go far beyond the utmost rigor of the law, and vent their savage cruelty upon him. It is with pain I have to communicate these things. But you may not hear them from him. I could not get to see him or them, as Vincennes is about thirty miles from Princeton, where I was when I heard of the capture.

I take pleasure in stating that, according to the letter he (Concklin) wrote to Mr. D. Stewart, Mr. Concklin did not abandon them, but risked his own liberty to save them. He was not with them when they were taken; but went afterwards to take them out of jail upon a writ of

56

Habeas Corpus, when they seized him too and lodged him in prison.

I write in much haste. If I can learn any more facts of importance, I may write you. If you desire to hear from me again, or if you should learn any thing specific from Mr. Concklin, be pleased to write me at Cincinnati, where I expect to be in a short time. If curious to know your correspondent, I may say I was formerly Editor of the "New Concord Free Press," Ohio. I only add that every case of this kind only tends to make me abhor my (no!) *this* country more and more. It is the Devil's Government, and God will destroy it.

Yours for the slave,
N. R. Johnston

P.S. I broke open this letter to write you some more. The foregoing pages were written at night. I expected to mail it next morning before leaving Evansville; but the boat for which I was waiting came down about three in the morning; so I had to hurry on board, bringing the letter along. As it now is I am not sorry, for coming down, on my way to St. Louis, as far as Paducah, there I learned from a colored man at the wharf that, that same day, in the morning, the master and the family of fugitives arrived off the boat, and had then gone on their journey to Tuscumbia, but that the "white man" (Mr. Concklin) had "got away from them" about twelve miles up the river. It seems he got off the boat some way, near or at Smithland, K., a town at the mouth of the Cumberland River. I presume the report is true, and hope he will finally escape, though I was also told that they were in pursuit of him. Would that the others had also escaped. Peter and Levin could have done so, I think, if they had had resolution. One of them rode a horse, he not tied either, behind the coach in which the others were. He followed apparently "contented and happy." From report, they told their master, and even their pursuers, before the master came, that Concklin had decoyed them away, they coming unwillingly. I write on a very unsteady boat.

Another report found its way into the papers describing the arrest and capture of a family of fugitive slaves. It went on to say that a man named "Miller"—the white man who led them off—had been found drowned, his hands and feet tied with chains, and his skull fractured. There remained no doubt now that the man was Concklin. And that his body, tied in irons, was buried upon the river bank.

To spare his sisters from finding out the truth about their brother in the papers, James McKim assumed the painful duty of breaking the news to them. He was acquainted with one of them—Mrs. Supplee—a true friend of the slave and a liberal giver to the Female Anti-slavery Society in Philadelphia.

By means of her strong will she was able to control the outward manifestations of grief, after the initial shock. She did not complain that he did not tell her of his dangerous journey south. She declared she would not have tried to stop him, for she would have failed even if she had tried. Now and again she fought tears as the memory of her brother's life came back to her in vivid recall. He had more than once offered his services to those in need—sacrificing his time and effort in their behalf.

The following extract from a letter sent by Reverend N. R. Johnston further clarified the episode:

My heart bleeds when I think of those poor, hunted and heart-broken fugitives, though a most interesting family, taken back to bondage ten fold worse than Egyptian. And then poor Concklin! How my heart expanded in love to him, as he told me his adventures, his trials, his toils, his fears and his hopes! After hearing all, and then seeing and communing with the family, now joyful in hopes of soon seeing their husband and father in the land of freedom; now in terror lest the human blood-hounds should be at their heels, I felt as though I could lay down my life in the cause of the oppressed. In that hour or two of intercourse with Peter's family, my heart warmed with love to them. I never saw more interesting young men. They would make Remonds or Douglasses, if they had the same opportunities.

While I was with them, I was elated with joy at their escape, and yet, when I heard their tale of woe, especially that of the mother, I could not suppress tears of deepest emotion.

My joy was short-lived. Soon I heard of their capture. The telegraph had been the means of their being claimed. I could have torn down all the telegraph wires in the land. It was a strange dispensation of Providence.

On Saturday the sad news of their capture came to my ears. We had resolved to go to their aid on Monday, as the trial was set for Thursday. On Sabbath, I spoke from Psalm xii.5. "For the oppression of the poor, for the sighing of the needy, now will I arise," saith the Lord: "I will set him in safety from him that puffeth at (from them that would enslave) him." When on Monday morning I learned that the fugitives had passed throught the place on Sabbath, and Concklin in chains, probably at the very time I was speaking on the subject referred to, my heart sank within me. And even yet, I cannot but exclaim, when I think of it—O, Father! how long ere Thou wilt arise to avenge the wrongs of the poor slave! Indeed, my dear brother, His ways are very mysterious. We have the consolation, however, to know that all is for the best. Our Redeemer does all things well. When He hung upon the cross, His poor broken hearted disciples could

59

not understand the providence; it was a dark time to them; and yet that was an event that was fraught with more joy to the world than anything that has occurred or could occur. Let us stand at our post and wait God's time. Let us have on the whole armor of God, and fight for the right, knowing, that though we may fall in battle, the victory will soon be ours, sooner or late. . . .

May God lead you into all truth, and sustain you in your labors, and fulfill your prayers and hopes. Adieu.

N. R. Johnston

Stunned by the horrible ending to all concerned, Peter hoped to contact a reliable person such as a merchant, lawyer, doctor, or planter—not too completely interlinked with slavery—to act as negotiator for the sale of his family. Efforts made through his brother by means of the Underground Railroad brought no immediate results. After a while, the following letter from the owner of his family came to the attention of William Still:

South Florence, Ala. 6 Augest, 1851

Mr. William Still *No. 31 North Fifth street Philadelphia*
Sir a few days sinc mr Lewis Tharenton of Tuscumbia Ala shewed me a letter dated 6 June 51 from cincinnati signd samuel Lewis in behalf of a Negro man by the name of peter Gist who informed the writer of the Letter that you ware his brother and wished an answer to be directed to you as he peter would be in philadelphi. the object of the letter was to purchis from me 4 Negros that is peters wife & 3 children, 2 sons & 1 girl the Name of said Negres are the woman Viney the (mother) Eldest son peter, 21 or 2 years old second son Leven 19 or 20 years 1 girl about 13 or 14 years old. the Husband & Father of these people once Belonged to a relation of mine by the name of Gist now Decest & some few

60

years since he peter was sold to a man by the Name of Freedman who removed to cincinnati ohio and Tuck peter with
him of course peter became free by the volentary act of the
master some time last march a white man by the name of
Miller apperd in the nabourhood & abducted the bove negroes was caut at vincanes Indi with said negroes & was
thare convicted of steling & remanded back to Ala to Abide
the penalty of the law & on his return met his Just reward by
getting drownded at the mouth of the cumberland River on
the ohio in attempting to make his escape I recovered and
Braught Back said 4 negroes or as you would say coulard
people under the Belief that peter the Husband was accessery
to the offence thereby putting me to much Expense & Truble
to the amt $1000 which if he gets them he or his Friends
must refund these four negroes are worth in the market about
4000 for thea are Extraordinary fine & likely & but for the
fact of Elopement I would not take 8000 Dollars for them
but as the thing now stands you can say to peter and his new
discovered Relations in philadelphia I will take 5000 for the
4 culerd people & if this will suite him & he can raise the
money I will delever to him or his agent at paduca at
mouth of Tennessee river said negroes but the money must
be Deposeted in the Hands of some respectabl person at
paduca before I remove the property it would not be safe for
peter to come to this countery write me a line on recpt of
this & let me Know peters views on the above

I am Yours &c
B. McKiernon

N B say to peter to write & let me Know his viewes
amediately as I am determined to act in a way if he dont
take this offer he will never have an other opportunity

B. McKiernon

Hoping to bargain with the slave owner, William wrote:

61

To B. McKiernon, Esq.: *Sir*—I have received your letter from South Florence, Ala., under date of the 6th inst. To say that it took me by surprise, as well as afforded me pleasure, for which I feel to be very much indebted to you, is no more than true. In regard to your informants of myself— Mr. Thornton, of Ala., and Mr. Samuel Lewis, of Cincinnati —to them both I am a stranger. However, I am the brother of Peter, referred to, and with the fact of his having a wife and three children in your service I am also familiar. This brother, Peter, I have only had the pleasure of knowing for the brief space of one year and thirteen days, although he is now past forty, and I twenty-nine years of age. Time will not allow me at present, or I should give you a detailed account of how Peter became a slave, the forty long years which intervened between the time he was kidnapped, when a boy, being only six years of age, and his arrival in this city, from Alabama, one year and fourteen days ago, when he was re-united to his mother, five brothers and three sisters.

None but a father's heart can fathom the anguish and sorrows felt by Peter during the many vicissitudes through which he has passed. He looked back to his boyhood and saw himself snatched from the tender embraces of his parents and home to be made a slave for life.

During all his prime days he was in the faithful and constant service of those who had no just claim upon him. In the meanwhile he married a wife, who bore him eleven children, the greater part of whom were emancipated from the troubles of life by death, and three only survived. To them and his wife he was devoted. Indeed I have never seen attachment between parents and children, or husband and wife, more entire than was manifested in the case of Peter.

Through these many years of servitude, Peter was sold and resold, from one State to another, from one owner to

62

another, till he reached the forty-ninth year of his age, when, in a good Providence, through the kindness of a friend and the sweat of his brow, he regained the God-given blessings of liberty. He eagerly sought his parents and home with all possible speed and pains, when, to his heart's joy, he found his relatives.

Your present humble correspondent is the youngest of Peter's brothers, and the first one of the family he saw after arriving in this part of the country. I think you could not fail to be interested in hearing how we became known to each other, and the proof of our being brothers, etc., all of which I should be most glad to relate, but time will not permit me to do so. The news of this wonderful occurrence, of Peter finding his kindred, was published quite extensively, shortly afterwards, in various newspapers, in this quarter, which may account for the fact of "Miller's" knowledge of the whereabouts of the "fugitives." Let me say, it is my firm conviction that no one had any hand in persuading "Miller" to go down from Cincinnati, or any other place, after the family. As glad as I should be, and as much as I would do for the liberation of Peter's family (now no longer young), and his three "likely" children, in whom he prides himself—how much, if you are a father, you can imagine; yet, I would not, and could not, think of persuading any friend to peril his life, as would be the case, in an errand of that kind.

As regards the price fixed upon by you for the family, I must say I do not think it possible to raise half that amount, though Peter authorized me to say he would give you twenty-five hundred for them. Probably he is not as well aware as I am, how difficult it is to raise so large a sum of money from the public. The applications for such objects are so frequent among us in the North, and have always been so liberally met, that it is no wonder if many get tired of being called upon. To be sure some of us brothers own some property, but no great amount; certainly not enough to enable us to bear so great a burden. Mother owns a small farm in New Jersey, on which she has lived for nearly forty years, from which she derives her support in her old age. This small farm contains between forty and fifty acres, and is the fruit of my father's toil. Two of my brothers own small places also, but they have young families, and consequently consume nearly as much as they make, with the exception of adding some improvements to their places.

For my own part, I am employed as a clerk for a living, but my salary is quite too limited to enable me to contribute any great amount towards so large a sum as is demanded. Thus you see how we are situated financially. We have plenty of friends, but little money. Now, sir, allow me to make an appeal to your humanity, although we are aware of your power to hold as property those poor slaves, mother, daughter and two sons,—that in no part of the United States could they escape and be secure from your claim—nevertheless, would your understanding, your heart, or your conscience reprove you, should you restore to them, without price, that dear freedom, which is theirs by right of nature, or would you not feel a satisfaction in so doing which all the wealth of the world could not equal? At all events, could you not so reduce the price as to place it in the power of Peter's relatives and friends to raise the means for their purchase? At first, I doubt not, but that you will think my appeal very unreasonable; but, sir, serious reflection will decide, whether the money demanded by you, after all, will be of as great a benefit to you, as the satisfaction you would find in bestowing so great a favor upon those whose entire happiness in this life depends mainly upon your decision in the matter. If the entire family cannot be purchased or freed, what can Vina and her daughter be purchased for? Hoping, sir, to

hear from you, at your earliest convenience, I subscribe myself,

Your obedient servant,
William Still

When months passed and he received no reply, William
Still knew his plea had been refused, that he would not be
able to buy the freedom of the family for less than the five
thousand dollars demanded by McKiernon.

chapter four

Although the rescue of his brother's children and wife preoccupied him, William Still and his associates at the Antislavery office found their attention drawn to a larger than usual number of slave abductions taking place in the North. Now came the greatest trials in regard to the Fugitive Slave Law.

Papers, speeches, and lectures against the law on grounds of inhumanity and godlessness appeared almost daily in antislavery groups. And to counteract this sentiment, proslavery adherents in the North sided with slaveholders in the South to compel obedience to the provisions of the bill. It came as no surprise that free black men in the state felt compelled to arm themselves in order to resist the intrusions of kidnappers who might come to capture them.

James Hamlet was the first case in which a man was arrested summarily under the Fugitive Slave Law. Hamlet was returned to bondage from the State of New York.

William and Ellen Craft were hotly pursued to Boston by hunters from Georgia.

Adam Gibson, a free colored man residing in Philadelphia, was arrested, delivered into the hands of his claimants by Commissioner Edward D. Ingraham, and hurried into slavery.

Euphemia Williams (the mother of six children) was a case which excited much interest although she foiled her captors.

A man named Shadrach was arrested and rescued in Boston.

Hannah Dellum and her child were returned to slavery from Philadelphia.

Thomas Hall and his wife were seized at midnight in Chester County, beaten, and dragged off to slavery.

One year after the passage of the law, at a time when alarm and excitement were running high, the most decided stand to defeat the law and defend freedom was taken at a town named Christiana in Pennsylvania. A group of slave-hunters were making arrangements in Philadelphia for the recapture of fugitive slaves. But fortunately for the fugitives, the plans of the slave-hunters and the local officials leaked out. Information about the plans was sent to the Anti-slavery office, and it, in turn, dispatched a messenger to Christiana to warn the persons involved.

But among those notified were brave hearts who refused to run away from the slave-catchers. They resolved to stand up for their rights. Indeed, they were prepared to fight to the death for them if the need arose.

The following report of the bloody contest that ensued was carefully written at the time by C. M. Burleigh, editor of the Pennsylvania *Freeman,* who visited the scene of battle immediately after it was over:

Last Thursday morning, (the 11th inst.), a peaceful neighborhood in the borders of Lancaster county was made the scene of a bloody battle, resulting from an attempt to capture seven colored men as fugitive slaves. As the reports of the affray which came to us were contradictory, and having good reason to believe that those of the daily press were grossly one-sided and unfair, we repaired to the scene of the tragedy, and, by patient inquiry and careful examination, endeavored to learn the real facts. To do this, from the varying and conflicting statements which we encountered, scarcely two of which agreed in every point, was not easy; but we believe the account we give below, as the result of these inquiries, is substantially correct.

Very early on the 11th inst. a party of slave-hunters went into a neighborhood about two miles west of Christiana, near the eastern border of Lancaster county, in pursuit of fugitive slaves. The party consisted of Edward Gorsuch, his son, Dickerson Gorsuch, his nephew, Dr. Pearce, Nicholas Hutchins, and others, all from Baltimore county, Md., and one Henry H. Kline, a notorious slave-catching constable from Philadelphia, who had been deputized by Commissioner Ingraham for this business. At about day-dawn they were discovered lying in an ambush near the house of one William Parker, a colored man, by an inmate of the house, who had started for his work. He fled back to the house, pursued by the slave-hunters, who entered the lower part of the house, but were unable to force their way into the upper part, to which the family had retired. A horn was blown from an upper window; two shots were fired, both, as we believe, though we are not certain, by the assailants, one at the colored men who fled into the house, and the other at the inmates, through the window. No one was wounded by either. A parley ensued. The slave-holder demanded his slaves, who he said were concealed in the house. The colored men presented themselves successively at the window, and asked if they were the slaves claimed; Gorsuch said, that neither of them was his slave. They told him that they were the only colored men in the house, and were determined never to be taken alive as slaves. Soon the colored people of the neighborhood, alarmed by the horn, began to gather, armed with guns, axes, corn-cutters, or clubs. Mutual threatenings were uttered by the two parties. The slave-holders told the blacks that resistance would be useless, as they had a party of thirty men in the woods nearby. The blacks warned them again to leave, as they would die before they would go into Slavery.

From an hour to an hour and a half passed in these parleyings, angry conversations, and threats; the blacks increasing by new arrivals, until they probably numbered from thirty to fifty, most of them armed in some way. About this time, Castner Hanaway, a white man, and a Friend, who resided in the neighborhood, rode up, and was soon followed by Elijah Lewis, another Friend, a merchant, in Cooperville, both gentlemen highly esteemed as worthy and peaceable citizens. As they came up, Kline, the deputy marshal, ordered them to aid him, as a United States officer, to capture the fugitive slaves. They refused of course, as would any man not utterly destitute of honor, humanity, and moral principle, and warned the assailants that it was madness for them to attempt to capture fugitive slaves there, or even to remain, and begged them if they wished to save their own lives, to leave the ground. Kline replied, "Do you really think so?" "Yes," was the answer, "the sooner you leave, the better, if you would prevent bloodshed." Kline then left the ground, retiring into a very safe distance into a cornfield, and toward the woods. The blacks were so exasperated by his threats, that, but for the interposition of the two white Friends, it is very doubtful whether he would have escaped without injury. Messrs. Hanaway and Lewis both exerted their influence to dissuade the colored people from violence, and would probably have succeeded in restraining them, had not the assailing party fired upon them. Young Gorsuch asked his father to leave, but the old man refused, declaring, as it is said and believed, that he would "go to hell, or have his slaves."

69

Finding they could do nothing further, Hanaway and Lewis both started to leave, again counselling the slave-hunters to go away, and the colored people to peace, but had gone but a few rods, when one of the inmates of the house attempted to come out at the door. Gorsuch presented his revolver, ordering him back. The colored man replied, "You had better go away, if you don't want to get hurt," and at the same time pushed him aside and passed out. Maddened at this, and stimulated by the question of his nephew, whether he would "take such an insult from a d—d nigger," Gorsuch fired at the colored man, and was followed by his son and nephew, who both fired their revolvers. The fire was returned by the blacks, who made a rush upon them at the same time. Gorsuch and his son fell, the one dead the other wounded. The rest of the party after firing their revolvers, fled precipitately through the corn and to the woods, pursued by some of the blacks. One was wounded, the rest escaped unhurt. Kline, the deputy marshal, who now boasts of his miraculous escape from a volley of musket-balls, had kept at a safe distance, though urged by young Gorsuch to stand by his father and protect him, when he refused to leave the ground. He of course came off unscathed. Several colored men were wounded, but none severely. Some had their hats or their clothes perforated with bullets; others had flesh wounds. They said that the Lord protected them, and they shook the bullets from their clothes. One man found several shot in his boot, which seemed to have spent their force before reaching him, and did not even break the skin. The slave-holders having fled, several neighbors, mostly Friends and anti-slavery men, gathered to succor the wounded and take charge of the dead. We are told that Parker himself protected the wounded man from his excited comrades, and brought water and a bed from his own house for the invalid, thus showing that he was as magnanimous to his fallen enemy as he was brave in the defence of his own liberty. The young man was then removed to a neighboring house, where the family received him with the tenderest kindness and paid him every attention, though they told him in Quaker phrase, that "they had no unity with his cruel business," and were very sorry to see him engaged in it. He was much affected by their kindness, and we are told, expressed his regret that he had been thus engaged, and his determination, if his life was spared, never again to make a similar attempt. His wounds are very severe, and it is feared mortal. All attempts to procure assistance to capture the fugitive slaves failed, the people in the neighborhood either not relishing the business of slave-catching, or at least, not choosing to risk their lives in it. There was a very great reluctance felt to going even to remove the body and the wounded man, until several abolitionists and Friends had collected for that object, when others found courage to follow on. The excitement caused by this most melancholy affair is very great among all classes. The abolitionists, of course, mourn the occurrence, while they see in it a legitimate fruit of the Fugitive Slave Law, just such a harvest of blood as they had long feared that the law would produce, and which they had earnestly labored to prevent. We believe that they alone, of all classes of the nation, are free from responsibility for its occurrence, having wisely foreseen the danger, and faithfully labored to avert it by removing its causes, and preventing the inhuman policy which has hurried on the bloody convulsion.

The enemies of the colored people, are making this the occasion of fresh injuries, and a more bitter ferocity toward that defenseless people, and of new misrepresentation and calumnies against the abolitionists.

The colored people, though the great body of them had no connection with this affair, are hunted like partridges

71

upon the mountains, by the relentless horde which has been poured forth upon them, under the pretense of arresting the parties concerned in the fight. When we reached Christiana, on Friday afternoon, we found that the Deputy-Attorney Thompson, of Lancaster, was there, and had issued warrants, upon the depositions of Kline and others, for the arrest of all suspected persons. A company of police were scouring the neighborhood in search of colored people, several of whom were seized while at their work near by, and brought in.

Castner Hanaway and Elijah Lewis, hearing that warrants were issued against them, came to Christiana, and voluntarily gave themselves up, calm and strong in the confidence of their innocence. They, together with arrested colored men, were sent to Lancaster jail that night.

The next morning we visited the ground of the battle, and the family where young Gorsuch now lives, and while there, we saw a deposition which he had just made, that he believed no white persons were engaged in the affray, besides his own party. As he was on the ground during the whole controversy, and deputy marshal Kline had discreetly run off into the corn-field, before the fighting began, the hireling slave-catcher's eager and confident testimony against our white friends, will, we think, weigh lightly with impartial men.

On returning to Christiana, we found that the United States Marshal from the city, had arrived at that place, accompanied by Commissioner Ingraham, Mr. Jones, a special commissioner of the United States, from Washington, and the U.S. District Attorney Ashmead, with forty-five U.S. Marines from the Navy Yard, and a posse of about forty of the City Marshal's police, together with a large body of special constables, eager for such a man-hunt, from Columbia and Lancaster and other places. The crowd divided into parties, of from ten to twenty-five, and scoured the country, in every direction, for miles around, ransacking the houses of the colored people, and captured every colored man they could find, with several colored women, and two other white men. Never did our heart bleed with deeper pity for the peeled and persecuted colored people, than when we saw this troop let loose upon them, and witnessed the terror and distress which its approach excited in families, wholly innocent of the charges laid against them.

The antislavery men, faced with dreadful opposition, read the following excerpt from one of Philadelphia's leading daily journals:

There can be no difference of opinion concerning the shocking affair which occurred at Christiana, on Thursday, the resisting of a law of Congress by a band of armed negroes, whereby the majesty of the Government was defied and life taken in one and the same act. There is something more than an ordinary, something more than even a murderous riot in all this. It is an act of insurrection, we might, considering the peculiar class and condition of the guilty parties, almost call it a servile insurrection—if not also one of treason. Fifty, eighty, or a hundred persons, whether white or black, who are deliberately in arms for the purpose of resisting the law, even the law for the recovery of fugitive slaves, are in the attitude of levying war against the United States; and doubly heavy becomes the crime of murder in such a case, and doubly serious the accountability of all who have any connection with the act as advisers, suggesters, countenancers, or accessories in any way whatever.

This paper represented the Whig party—the more moderate and respectable class of people.

But even the words of one of the leading democratic organs of Philadelphia confirmed the consensus opinion of the people:

We will not, however, insult the reader by arguing that which has not been heretofore doubted, and which is not doubted now, by ten honest men in the State, and that is that the abolitionists are implicated in the Christiana murder. All the ascertained facts go to show that they were the real, if not the chief instigators. White men are known to harbor fugitives, in the neighborhood of Christiana, and these white men are known to be abolitionists, known to be opposed to the Fugitive Slave Law, and *known* to be the warm friends of William F. Johnston, [Governor of the State of Pennsylvania]. And, as if to clinch the argument, no less than three white men are now in the Lancaster prison, and were arrested as accomplices in the dreadful affair on the morning of the eleventh. And one of these white men was committed on a charge of high treason, on Saturday last, by the United States Commissioner Ingraham.

This is the report of the affair by another daily—though of opposite political outlook:

The unwarrantable outrage committed last week, at Christiana, Lancaster county, is a foul stain upon the fair name and fame of our State. We are pleased to see that the officers of the Federal and State Governments are upon the tracks of those who were engaged in the riot, and that several arrests have been made.

We do not wish to see the poor misled blacks who participated in the affair, suffer to any extent, for they were but tools. The men who are really chargeable with treason against the United States Government, and with the death of Mr. Gorsuch, an estimable citizen of Maryland, are un-

74

questionably *white,* with hearts black enough to incite them to the commission of any crime equal in atrocity to that committed in Lancaster county. Pennsylvania has now but one course to pursue, and that is to aid, and warmly aid, the United States in bringing to condign punishment, every man engaged in the riot. She owes it to herself and to the Union. Let her in this resolve, be just and fearless.

Finally, the following excerpt is taken from a leading neutral daily paper:

One would suppose from the advice of forcible resistance, so familiarly given by the abolitionists, that they are quite unaware that there is any such crime as treason recognized by the Constitution, or punished with death by the laws of the United States. We would remind them, that not only is there such a crime, but that there is a solemn decision of the Supreme Court, that all who are concerned in a conspiracy which ripens into treason, whether present or absent from the scene of actual violence, are involved in the same liabilities as the immediate actors. If they engage in the conspiracy and stimulate the treason, they may keep their bodies from the affray without saving their necks from a halter.

It would be very much to the advantage of Society, if an example could be made of some of these agitators, who excite the ignorant and reckless to treasonable violence, from which they themselves shrink, but who are, not only in morals, but in law, equally guilty and equally amenable to punishment with the victims of their inflammatory counsels.

Public opinion brought the matter to a point which resulted in a petition presented to the Governor.

The undersigned, citizens of Pennsylvania, respectfully represent:

That citizens of a neighboring State have been cruelly assassinated by a band of armed outlaws at a place not more than three hours' journey distant from the seat of Government and from the commercial metropolis of the State:

That this insurrectionary movement in one of the most populous parts of the State has been so far successful as to overawe the local ministers of justice and paralyze the power of the law:

That your memorialists are not aware that "any military force" has been sent to the seat of insurrection, or that the civil authority has been strengthened by the adoption of any measures suited to the momentous crisis.

They, therefore, respectfully request the chief executive magistrate of Pennsylvania to take into consideration the necessity of vindicating the outraged laws, and sustaining the dignity of the Commonwealth on this important and melancholy occasion.

Public excitement ran high! Faced by an hour of crisis, antislavery men, as well as the fugitives they helped, despaired for the cause of freedom. The authorities of the State of Pennsylvania joined forces with those from Maryland to make a series of arrests wherever they suspected an accomplice could be found. Soon twenty-seven persons were taken into custody.

But this was just the beginning of the hysteria. Indeed, at the first day's hearing inquiring into the incident of Christiana, the atmosphere proved slightly entertaining. Present were two or three non-resistant Quakers and a number of poor defenseless colored women taken as prisoners. Standing over the distracted "criminals," the defenders of slavery prepared to charge them with levying war against the United States. In this way, the hearing took place solemnly in Lancaster.

Representing the Commonwealth were six leading attorneys headed by John L. Thompson, the District Attorney; George L. Ashmead, of Philadelphia, representing the United States authorities; and Robert Brent, Attorney General of Maryland.

The counsel for the defense was led by Thaddeus Stevens, a well-known antislavery lawyer from Philadelphia. He had four counselors to aid him.

This short extract of a report of the first day's hearing sets the stage:

> The excitement at Christiana, during yesterday, was very great. Several hundred persons were present, and the deepest feeling was manifested against the perpetrators of the outrage. At two o'clock yesterday afternoon, the United States Marshal, Mr. Roberts, United States District Attorney, J. H. Ashmead, Esq., Mr. Commissioner Ingraham, and Recorder Lee, accompanied by the United States Marines, returned to the city. . . .

The rest of the story told of the lodging of the prisoners in the jail cells to await trial for treason.

Referring to the events of the second day's affairs, the Philadelphia *Ledger* described the actual manhunt in which the accessories were apprehended and brought into custody.

With public sentiment a hundred to one against the fugitive slave, William Parker, now safe in Canada, his brave comrades who faced trial, and their counsel, led by the indomitable Thaddeus Stevens, prepared to fight.

As the weeks passed by, public feeling shifted from a cry for the life of the killer of Gorsuch, the slaveholder—although the death was still deplored—to an awakening sympathy with the defendants. Hundreds even came to visit the prisoners in their cells to cheer them in the dark time.

And even more than this, two of the prisoners who had been identified in the jail as fugitive slaves by their masters, escaped mysteriously. It was strongly suspected they were helped on their way by one of the United States Marshals— A. E. Roberts. At any rate, when the day of the trial approached, their cell was empty.

Judge Kane made the charge of treason. Ashmead, Attorney of the United States for the Eastern District of Pennsylvania, presented to the Grand Jury a copy of the indictment against the offenders. With true bills found against them, their names were inserted in separate copies of the indictment.

The abolitionists, in turn, left no stone unturned to meet the case in court. During this interim, many tokens of kindness and Christian charity were heaped upon the prisoners by their friends. Thomas L. Kane, son of the judge, saw that a sumptuous Thanksgiving dinner was served them. It consisted of turkey, and all the traditional dishes, including a delicious pound cake for dessert. The dinner for the white prisoners was served in the room of Mr. Morrison, one of the keepers. Marshal Roberts, several of the keepers, and Mr. Hanes, one of the prison officers, chatted with Messrs. Hanaway, Davis, and Scarlett—the white men awaiting trial—as did the Mayor of Philadelphia, Charles Gilpin.

Mrs. Martha Hanaway, the wife of the "traitor" of that name, had spent most of her time with her husband since his incarceration. On that day she served each of the twenty-seven colored "traitors" with a plate of food. And with plenty left over, she fed the outsiders in the other cells on the same corridor.

When word leaked to the proslavery party, they became indignant. Mr. Brent complained to the court about the festivities permitted the prisoners. Most of all, they worried about the antislavery sympathies shown by the judge's son.

Castner Hanaway was the first to stand trial. The great contest would be made over this white man. Thaddeus Stevens prepared to fight for his freedom, while District Attorney Ashmead stood firm against the "traitors."

The prisoners had lain in the cells for three long months before the day of trial began. But then, on Monday morning, November 24th, a jury was selected.

After picking the jury, the battle began in earnest and continued for nearly two weeks. Examinations and cross-examinations were followed by arguments and counter-arguments. It became evident that this was the most important trial involving Underground Railroad passengers that had yet taken place in the country.

Aware of the significance of the outcome of the trial, antislavery lawyers were determined to cut through the allegations of the prosecution. The shaky foundations of Brent and his adherents buckled under the brilliant rebuttals of Stevens. The theory of "treason" was swept away, thereby weakening the proslavery case.

Slowly the tide of opinion shifted. Hanaway and the other "traitors" took on the aspect of injured men. The enemy, demoralized, lost face.

Hanaway was victorious!

Then the effort was made to convict Thompson, one of the colored "traitors."

He, too, was pronounced "not guilty." And the others met the same good fortune.

The victory was complete. Underground Railroad "stock" rose considerably. The Anti-slavery office in Philadelphia could now feel more secure about the safety of any fugitives it would help.

chapter five

The time had come to reorganize the Anti-slavery Society of Philadelphia. Slaveholders plagued the courts in the city to return their slaves; and, although the abolitionists had won in the Christiana case and in several other battles, they did not underestimate the foe.

A Vigilance Committee had operated in the past out of the old Pennsylvania Society for the Abolition of Slavery. Its primary function was to keep alert to meet any runaway slave lucky enough to cross Mason and Dixon's line. Its activities were known only to the "elect" and consisted mainly of helping the slave on to Canada. In addition, it sounded the alarm when slave-catchers arrived in the city.

In order to tighten the organization, and to form a stronger Vigilance Committee, a motion was made which was published in the Pennsylvania *Freeman* of December 9, 1852. It read as follows:

> Pursuant to the motion published in last week's *Freeman,* a meeting was held in the Anti-slavery rooms, on the evening of the 2nd inst., for the purpose of organizing a Vigilance Committee.

On motion Samuel Nickless was appointed chairman, and William Still secretary. J. M. McKim then stated . . . that the friends of the fugitive slave had been for some years past, embarrassed, for the want of a properly constructed active, Vigilance Committee; that the old Committee, which used to render effective service in this field of Anti-slavery labor, had become disorganized and scattered, and that for the last two or three years the duties of this department had been performed by individuals on their own responsibility, and sometimes in a very irregular manner; that this had been the cause of much dissatisfaction and complaint, and that the necessity for a remedy of this state of things was generally felt. Hence, the call for this meeting. It was intended now to organize a committee, which should be composed of persons of known responsibility, and who could be relied upon to act systematically and promptly, and with the least possible expenditure of money in all cases that might require their attention.

James Mott and Samuel Nickless, expressed their hearty concurrence in what had been said, as did also B. N. Goines and N. W. Depee. The opinion was also expressed by one or more of these gentlemen, that the organization to be formed should be of the simplest possible character; with no more machinery or officers than might be necessary to hold it together and keep it in proper working order. After some discussion, it was agreed first to form a general committee, with a chairman, whose business it should be to call meetings when necessity should seem to require it, and to preside at the same; and a treasurer to take charge of the funds; and second, to appoint out of this general committee an acting committee of four persons, who should have the responsibility of attending to every case that might require their aid, as well as the exclusive authority to raise the funds necessary for their purpose. It was further agreed that it should be the duty of the chairman of the Acting Committee to keep a

81

record of all their doings, and especially of the money received and expended on behalf of every case claiming their interposition.

Under the heading, General Vigilance Committee, nineteen prominent antislavery workers from Philadelphia were listed, including: James McKim, Robert Purvis, Charles Bustill, Samuel Nickless, Charles Wise, William Still, Passmore Williamson, and Jacob White, among others.

The article went on to read:

Robert Purvis was understood to be Chairman of the General Committee, having been nominated at the head of the list, and Charles Wise was appointed treasurer. The Acting Committee was thus constituted:

William Still, chairman, N. W. Depee, Passmore Williamson, and J. C. White. This Committee was appointed for the term of one year.

On motion, the proceedings of this meeting were ordered to be published in the Pennsylvania *Freeman.*

(Adjourned.)

William Still, Secretary.   Samuel Nickless, Chairman.

The Committee having been organized, J. M. McKim, Corresponding Secretary and General Agent of the Pennsylvania Anti-slavery Society, issued the subjoined notice which was published shortly afterward in the Pennsylvania *Freeman,* and the colored churches throughout the city:

We are pleased to see that we have at last, what has for some time been felt to be a desideratum in Philadelphia, a responsible and duly authorized Vigilance Committee. The duties of this department of Anti-slavery labor, have, for want of such an organization, been performed in a very loose and unsystematic manner. The names of the persons constituting the Acting Committee, are a guarantee that this will not be the case hereafter. They are—

William Still (Chairman),	31 North Fifth Street,
Nathaniel W. Depee,	334 South Street,
Jacob C. White,	100 Old York Road, and
Passmore Williamson,	southwest cor. Seventh and Arch Streets.

We respectfully commend these gentlemen, and the cause in which they are engaged, to the confidence and co-operation of all the friends of the hunted fugitive. Any funds contributed to any of them, or placed in the hands of their Treasurer, Charles Wise, corner of Fifth and Market Streets, will be sure of a faithful and judicious appropriation.

The new Chairman, William Still, was anxious to begin his duties. For some time he had been acutely aware of the importance of keeping detailed records of runaway slaves. His brother Peter, who came to him for help in finding his people, served to point this out. He thought how easy it would have been for the freed slave to ask for his mother and father if someone had written the names of the fugitives in a journal or record book. Suppose he had not been a clerk at the Anti-slavery office when Peter Still came through?

Still's other duties consisted of accounting for the small sums of money available to him and the other Committee members to feed and clothe the fugitives when they arrived hungry and often in rags. He was to find them lodgings for the nights they lingered in the city before being sent to Canada via the Underground Railroad.

Another part of his work was to advertise antislavery meetings and to see to the printing of handbills warning fugitives of slave-hunters and their agents who arrived in the city in hot pursuit of their "property."

He read proslavery newspapers such as the Richmond

Daily Dispatch and the Baltimore *Sun* to learn what runaway slaves were being sought, because often these same runaways arrived in Philadelphia.

Still conceived of a way to save the Society the small sums of money allotted for feeding and sheltering the slave —five to twenty dollars, in most cases. He'd have them stay at his house, sharing the bed and board he and his wife were only too glad to contribute free of charge.

Still and the other members of the Acting Committee— Passmore Williamson, whose face resembled his white Quaker father more than his colored mother, White, and Depee vowed to work day and night for the care of the hunted slaves who were arriving in larger and larger numbers every month.

Soon letters began to reach William Still, and the eager worker saved each piece of correspondence regarding runaway slaves. He kept a journal, or record book, in which he inscribed the details of the former life of the slaves who arrived at his Philadelphia office. He opened each letter carefully, made neat notations of the contents on the outside of the envelope for quick reference, and filed the letter away.

Before he became Secretary, the records had been scanty. But as the months passed, and he interviewed the former bondsmen, his records contained information of their former life which are typified by these accounts:

PERRY JOHNSON, OF ELKTON, MARYLAND.

Perry's exit was in November, 1853. He was owned by Charles Johnson, who lived at Elkton. . . . Perry had the misfortune to let a "load of fodder upset," about which his master became exasperated, and in his agitated state of mind he succeeded in affixing a number of very ugly station-

84

ary marks on Perry's back. However, this was no new thing. Indeed, he had suffered at the hands of his mistress even far more keenly than from those "ugly marks." He had but one eye; the other he had been deprived of by a terrible stroke with a cowhide in the "hand of his mistress." This lady he pronounced to be "a perfect savage.". . . Perry was about twenty-eight years of age and a man of promise. The Committee attended to his wants and forwarded him on North.

ISAAC FORMAN, WILLIAM DAVIS, AND WILLIS REDICK.

These passengers all arrived together, concealed, per steamship City of Richmond, December, 1853. Isaac Forman, the youngest of the party, about twenty-three years of age and a dark mulatto. . . . He fled from a widow by the name of Mrs. Sanders, who had been in the habit of hiring him out for "one hundred and twenty dollars a year." She belonged in Norfolk, Va., where Isaac served in the capacity of steward on the steamship Augusta. His wife lived in Richmond preventing him from seeing her much. "Once or twice in the year was all the privilege allowed" him to visit her. He placed no particular charges against his mistress when interviewed by the Committee. He went to Canada.

Willis Redick, came from Portsmouth, Va., and was owned by a merchant—S. J. Wilson. Willis was of a very dark hue, thick set, thirty-two years of age, and possessed of a fair share of mind. He was hired out for "one hundred dollars a year." Willis thought his lot "pretty hard," and his master became more severe in his treatment of the slave, finally "threatening" to sell him. He had enjoyed, as far as it was possible for a slave to enjoy, "five months of married life." In fact, he had just begun to consider what it was to have a wife and children that he "could not own or protect," and who were claimed as another's property. He left without consulting his master—or his wife.

This step looked exceedingly hard, but what else could

the poor fellow do? If he stayed his soul would have been crushed and his heart broken.

William Davis might be described as a good-looking mulatto, thirty-one years of age, and capable of thinking for himself. He made no grave complaints of ill-usage under his master, "Joseph Reynolds," who lived at Newton, Portsmouth, Va. However, his owner had occasionally "threatened to sell him." As this was too much for William's sensitive feelings, he took umbrage at it and made a hasty and hazardous move, which resulted in finding himself on the U.G.R.R. [Underground Rail Road]. The most serious regret William had to report to the Committee was, that he was compelled to "leave" his "wife," Catherine, and his little daughter, Louisa, two years and one month, and an infant son seven months old. He evidently loved them very tenderly, but saw no way by which he could aid them, as long as he was daily liable to be put on the auction block and sold far South. This argument was regarded by the Committee as logical and unanswerable; consequently they readily endorsed his course, while they deeply sympathized with his poor wife and little ones. "Before escaping," he "dared not" even apprise his wife and child, whom he had to leave behind in the prison house.

JOSEPH HENRY CAMP.

In November, 1853, in the twentieth year of his age, Camp was held to "service or labor" in the City of Richmond, Va., by Dr. K. Clark. Being uncommonly smart and quite good-looking at the same time, he was a saleable piece of merchandise. Without consulting his view of the matter . . . the master one day struck up a bargain with a trader for Joseph, and received *Fourteen Hundred Dollars cash* in consideration thereof. Mr. Robert Parrett, of Parson & King's Express office, happened to have a knowledge of what had transpired, and thinking pretty well of Joseph, confidentially put him in full possession of all the facts in the case. For reflection he hardly had five minutes. But he at once resolved to strike that day for freedom—not to go home that evening to be delivered into the hands of his new master. . . . He secreted himself, and so remained for three weeks. In the meantime, his mother, who was a slave, resolved to escape also, but after one week's gloomy foreboding, she became "faint-hearted and gave the struggle over." But Joseph did not know what surrender meant. His sole thought was to procure a ticket on the U.G.R.R. [Underground Rail Road] for Canada, which by persistent effort he succeeded in doing. He hid himself in a steamer, and by this means, reached Philadelphia, where he received every accommodation at the usual depot, was provided with a free ticket, and sent off rejoicing for Canada. His unfortunate mother was "detected and sold South."

The following notation was made by the energetic new Secretary in the ledger:

EX-PRESIDENT TYLER'S HOUSEHOLD LOSES AN ARISTOCRATIC "ARTICLE."

James Hambleton Christian is a remarkable specimen of the "well fed, &c." In talking with him relative to his life as a slave, he said very promptly, "I have always been treated well; if I only have half as good times in the North as I have had in the South, I shall be perfectly satisfied. Any time I desired spending money, five or ten dollars were no object." At times James had borrowed of his master, one, two, and three hundred dollars, to loan out to some of his friends. With regard to apparel and jewelry, he had worn the best, as an every-day adornment. With regard to food also, he had fared as well as heart could wish, with abundance of leisure time at his command. His deportment was certainly very re-fined and gentlemanly. About fifty per cent. of Anglo-Saxon blood was visible in his features and his hair, which gave him no inconsiderable claim to sympathy and care. He had been to William and Mary's College in his younger days, to wait on young master James B.C., where, through the kindness of some of the students, he had picked up a trifling amount of book learning. To be brief, this man was born the slave of old Major Christian, on the Glen Plantation, Charles City county, Va. The Christians were wealthy and owned many slaves and belonged in reality to the F.F.V.'s [First Families of Virginia]. On the death of the old Major, James fell into the hands of his son, Judge Christian, who was executor to his father's estate. Subsequently, he fell into the hands of one of the Judge's sisters, Mrs. John Tyler (wife of Ex-President Tyler), and then he became a member of the President's domestic household, was at the White House, under the President, from 1841 to 1845.

After a lapse of time, his mistress died. According to her request, after this event, James and his old mother were handed over to her nephew, William H. Christian, Esq., a merchant of Richmond. From this gentleman, James had the folly to flee.

Passing hurriedly over the interesting details, received from him respecting his remarkable history, two or three more incidents too good to omit must suffice.

"How did you like Mr. Tyler?" said an inquisitive member of the Vigilance Committee.

"I didn't like Mr. Tyler much," was the reply.

"Why?" again inquired a member of the Committee.

"Because Mr. Tyler was a poor man. I never did like poor people. I didn't like his marrying into our family, who were considered very far Tyler's superiors. On the plantation, Tyler was a very cross man, and treated the servants very cruelly; but the house servants were treated much better, owing to their having belonged to his wife, who protected them from persecution, as they had been favorite servants in her father's family." James estimated that "Tyler got

88

about thirty-five thousand dollars and twenty-nine slaves, young and old, by his wife."

What prompted James to leave such pleasant quarters? It was this: He had become enamored of a young and respectable free girl in Richmond, with whom he could not be united in marriage solely because he was a slave, and did not own himself. The frequent sad separations of such married couples (where one or the other was a slave) could not be overlooked; consequently, the poor fellow concluded that he would stand a better chance of gaining his object in Canada than by remaining in Virginia. So he began to feel that he might himself be sold some day, and thus the resolution came home to him very forcibly to make tracks for Canada.

In speaking of the good treatment he had always met with, a member of the Committee remarked, "You must be akin to some of your master's family?"

To which he replied, "I am Christian's son."

Unquestionably this passenger was one of that happy class so commonly referred to by apologists for the "Patriarchal Institution." The Committee, feeling a deep interest in his story, and desiring great success to him in his Underground efforts to get rid of slavery, and at the same time possess himself of his affianced, made him heartily welcome, feeling assured that the struggles and hardships he had submitted to in escaping, as well as the luxuries he was leaving behind, were nothing to be compared with the blessings of liberty and a free wife in Canada.

Not only did the new Chairman of the Acting Committee meet his fellow black men face to face, but he was given access to the many letters that poured in from the various "stations" of the Underground Railroad. Soon the handwriting of Thomas Garrett, the devoted friend of the slave who worked as "station-master" out of Wilmington, Delaware, became familiar at the Anti-slavery office. Indeed, the Quaker abolitionist had served long in the cause, and the fugitives he had fed and sheltered in his house grew to a large number—so large, in fact, that the brave white man had been tried in a U.S. court for aiding and abetting the fugitive slave. Because of his trial, at which time he was fined so heavily for damages that all of his property was swept away, he pledged to work even harder in the future in the aid of runaways. Friends were loyal to him and after a while he began to rebuild his retail business, though in his sixtieth year. As his antislavery activities had been advertised by the trial, the demand now became so great for shelter that he was compelled to put another story on his back buildings.

This letter from Garrett announced the arrival of "Moses" with six passengers:

Wilmington, 12 mo. 29th, 1854

Esteemed Friend, J. Miller McKim:—We made arrangements last night, and sent away Harriet Tubman, with six men and one woman to Allen Agnew's, to be forwarded across the country to the city. Harriet, and one of the men had worn their shoes off their feet, and I gave them two dollars to help fit them out, and directed a carriage to be hired at my expense, to take them out, but do not yet know the expense. I now have two more from the lowest county in Maryland, on the Peninsula, upwards of one hundred miles. I will try to get one of our trusty colored men to take them to-morrow morning to the Anti-slavery office. You can pass them on.

Thomas Garrett

"Moses" was the nickname of Harriet Tubman, this heroic black woman—herself a runaway slave—who went down into "Egypt" and who had delivered these six bonds-

90

men through her trusted friend's place in Wilmington and on to the North. All the antislavery men in that area respected the brave woman who had no pretensions—indeed, who was a very ordinary looking specimen of humanity, herself. So much so that it would have been hard to differentiate her from the unfortunate-appearing farm hands seen anywhere in the South. Yet, in point of courage, shrewdness, and self-disregarding motives she was unparalleled. Many was the time she went into Maryland on the Underground Railroad, during which interval she would be absent from her friends who understood she was planning a mission for yet another party of passengers. Great fears were entertained for her safety, but she seemed wholly devoid of personal fear. That she might be captured by slaveholders or slave-hunters never entered her mind. But while she manifested this lack of concern for her own safety, she was watchful with regard to the safety of those whom she piloted.

Half the time she displayed the demeanor of one asleep, and would actually sit down on the side of the road and go fast asleep when engaged in her errands of mercy. Yet she would not allow one of her party to whimper about "giving out and going back," however wearied he might become after a hard day or night of travel. In any emergency she gave all to understand that "times were very critical and therefore no foolishness would be indulged in on the road." That several who were weak-kneed and fainthearted became greatly invigorated by Harriet's blunt and positive manner and threat of extreme measures, there was little room to doubt.

After having enlisted, "they had to go through or die." Of course, Harriet was supreme and her followers generally had full faith in her, and would back up any word she might utter. Therefore, when she said to them, "A live runaway could do great harm by going back, but a dead one could tell no tales," she was sure to have obedience. Luckily, none had to die on the "middle passage." It was obvious that her success in going into Maryland as she did was attributable to her adventurous spirit and utter disregard of consequences. Her like was seldom seen before or since.

On December 29th, 1854, William Still recorded the arrival of these six passengers:

JOHN is twenty years of age, chestnut color, of spare build and smart. He fled from a farmer, by the name of John Campbell Henry, who resided at Cambridge, Dorchester Co., Maryland. On being interrogated as to the character of his master, John . . . testified that he was a "hard man" and that he "owned about one hundred and forty slaves and sometimes he would sell," etc. John was one of the slaves who were "hired out." He "desired to have the privilege of hunting his own master." His desire was not granted. Instead of meekly submitting, John felt wronged, and made this his reason for running away. This looked pretty spirited on the part of one so young as John. The Committee's respect for him was not a little increased, when they heard him express himself.

BENJAMIN was twenty-eight years of age, chestnut color, medium size, and shrewd. He was the so-called property of Eliza Ann Brodins, who lived near Buckstown, in Maryland. Ben did not hesitate to say, in unqualified terms, that his mistress was "very devilish." He considered his charges, proved by the fact that three slaves (himself one of them) were required to work hard and fare meagerly, to support his mistress' family in idleness and luxury. The Committee paid due attention to his ex parte statement, and was obliged to conclude that his argument, clothed in common and homely language, was forcible, if not eloquent, and that he was well worthy of aid. Benjamin left his parents besides one sister, Mary Ann Williamson, who wanted to come away on the Underground Rail Road.

HENRY left his wife, Harriet Ann, to be known in the future by the name of "Sophia Brown." He was a fellow-servant of Ben's, and one of the supports of Eliza A. Brodins.

HENRY was only twenty-two, but had quite an insight into matters and things going on among slaves and slave-holders generally, in country life. He was the father of two small children, whom he had to leave behind.

PETER was owned by George Wenthrop, a farmer, living near Cambridge, Md. In answer to the question, how he had been used, he said "hard." Not a pleasant thought did he entertain respecting his master, save that he was no longer to demand the sweat of Peter's brow. Peter left parents, who were free; he was born before they were emancipated; consequently, he was retained in bondage.

JANE, aged twenty-two, instead of regretting that she had unadvisedly left a kind mistress and indulgent master, who afforded her necessary comforts, affirmed that her master, "Rash Jones, was the worst man in the country." The Committee was at first disposed to doubt her sweeping statement, but when they heard particularly how she had been treated, they thought [she] had good ground for all that she said. Personal abuse and hard usage, were the common lot of poor slave girls.

ROBERT was thirty-five years of age, of a chestnut color, and well made. His report was similar to that of many others. He had been provided with plenty of drudgery—hewing of wood and drawing of water, and had hardly been treated as well as a gentleman would treat a dumb brute. His feelings, therefore, on leaving his old master and home, were those of an individual who had been unjustly in prison for a dozen years and had at last regained his liberty.

The civilization, religion, and customs under which Robert

and his companions had been raised, were, he thought "very wicked." Although these travelers were all of the field-hand order, they were, nevertheless, very promising, and they anticipated better days in Canada. Good advice was proffered them on the subject of temperance, industry, education, etc. Clothing, food and money were also given them to meet their wants, and they were sent on their way rejoicing.

While many sympathized with the slave, or gave money to help buy his freedom, only a precious few could be found who were willing to take the risk of going into the South and standing face to face with slavery in order to conduct a slave to freedom. In most cases, the undertaking was too fearful even to consider. But there were instances when men, and women too, moved by the love of freedom, would take their lives in their hands and nobly rescue the oppressed. Such an instance is found in the case of Matilda Mahoney, in Baltimore.

She was twenty-one years of age in 1854, when she escaped and came to Philadelphia, a handsome young woman, of a light complexion, quite refined in her manners, and possessing great personal attractions. But her situation as a slave had been critical.

Her claimant was William Rigard, of Frederick, Maryland, who hired her out to a Mr. Reese, in Baltimore; in this situation her duties were general housework and nursing. She was not so much dissatisfied with these labors as with the fact that her old master was tottering on the verge of the grave, and his son was a trader in New Orleans. These facts kept Matilda in extreme anxiety. For two years prior to her escape, the young trader had been trying to influence his father to let him have her for the Southern market; but the old man had never consented. The trader knew quite well that an "article" of her appearance would command a high price in the New Orleans market. But Matilda's attractions had won the heart of a young man in the North, one who had known her in Baltimore in earlier days, and this lover was willing to make desperate efforts to release her from her perilous situation. Whether or not he had nerve enough to venture down to Baltimore to accompany his intended on the Underground Railroad, his presence would not have aided the case. He had, however, a friend who offered to go to Baltimore on this desperate mission. The friend was James Jefferson of Providence, Rhode Island. With the strategy of a skilled soldier, Mr. Jefferson hurried to Baltimore, and almost under the eyes of the slaveholders and slave-catchers seized his prize and hurried her away on the Underground Railroad before her owner even discovered her escape. At Matilda's arrival at the station in Philadelphia, several other passengers from different points also happened to arrive, giving great anxiety to the Committee. Among these were a man and his wife and four children, from Maryland. Likewise an interesting and intelligent young girl who had been almost miraculously rescued from Norfolk, and in addition to these, the brother of J. W. Pennington, a New York minister, with his two sons.

While it was a great satisfaction to have the travelers arriving in such numbers, and especially to observe in every face, determination, rare manly and womanly bearing, and remarkable intelligence, it must be admitted that members of the Acting Committee felt at the same time a very lively dread of the slave-hunters and were constantly on their guard. Arrangements were made to send the fugitives on by different trains and in various directions. Matilda and all the others, with the exception of the father and two sons (relatives of Dr. Pennington), successfully escaped. In the case of the father and his sons, however, the outcome was different, despite the precautions taken. William Still informed Dr. Pennington of the good news of the coming of his kin, whom he had not seen for many, many years, and, in reply, received the following letter:

29 6th Avenue, New York, May 24th, 1854

My Dear Mr. Still:—Your kind letter of the 22nd inst. has come to hand and I have to thank you for your offices of benevolence to my bone and my flesh. I have had the pleasure of doing a little for your brother Peter, but I do not think it an offset. My burden has been great about these brethren. I hope they have started on to me. Many thanks, my good friend. Yours Truly.

J. W. C. Pennington

This letter intensified the deep interest which the Committee already felt in this matter and, at the same time, made clear their duty with regard to forwarding the doctor's brother and his sons to New York. Immediately, therefore, they were furnished with free tickets and were cautioned to be as careful as possible with regard to slave-hunters, if encountered on the road. In company with several other Underground Railroad passengers, and under the care of an intelligent guide, all were sent off in due order, looking quite as respectable as the most affluent of their race from any part of the country. The Committee in New York, with the doctor, were on the lookout, of course; and without difficulty all arrived safely.

Perhaps the arrival of his brother so overpowered the doctor that he forgot how imminent their danger was. Few could realize, even in imagination, the feelings that filled their hearts as the doctor and his brother reverted to their boyhood, when they were both slaves together in Maryland.

They recalled their separation through the escape of the former many years previous and marveled over the contrast, one elevated to a Doctor of Divinity, a scholar and noted clergyman well known in the United States and Great Britain, while at the same time, his brother and kin were held in chains and compelled to do unrequited labor—to come and go at the bidding of another. These thoughts would certainly be enough to distract the doctor for the moment from cool thought concerning slave-hunters. Only twenty-four hours after their arrival, and while resting their fatigued bodies in bed, just before daybreak, like a band of hyenas, the slave-hunters pounced upon all three of them, and soon had them handcuffed and hurried off to a U.S. Commissioner's office. Armed with the Fugitive Slave Law, and a strong guard of officers to carry it out, resistance would simply have been useless. Before the morning sun arose the telegraph bore the sad news to all parts of the country of an awful calamity on the Underground Railroad.

The Liberator reported the tragedy as follows:

THREE FUGITIVE SLAVES ARRESTED IN NEW YORK, AND GIVEN UP TO THEIR OWNERS.

New York, May 25th

About three o'clock this morning, three colored men, father and two sons, known as Jake, Bob, and Stephen Pennington, were arrested at the instance of David Smith and Jacob Grove, of Washington Co., Md., who claimed them as their slaves. They were taken before Commissioner Morton, of the United States Court, and it was understood that they would be examined at 11 o'clock; instead of that, however, the case was heard at once, no persons being present, when the claimants testified that they were the owners of said slaves and that they escaped from their service at Baltimore, on Sunday last.

From what we can gather of the proceedings, the fugitives acknowledged themselves to be slaves of Smith and Grove. The commissioner considering the testimony sufficient, ordered their surrender, and they were accordingly given up to their claimants, who hurried them off at once, and they are now on their way to Baltimore. A telegraph despatch has been sent to Philadelphia, as it is understood an attempt will be made to rescue the parties, when the cars arrive. There was no excitement around the commissioner's office, owing to a misunderstanding as to the time of examination. The men were traced to this city by the claimants, who made application to the United States Court, when officers Horton and De Angeles were deputied by the marshal to effect their arrest, and those officers, with deputy Marshal Thompson scoured the city, and finally found them secreted in a house in Broome Street. They were brought before Commissioner Morton this morning. No counsel appeared for the fugitives. The case being made out, the usual affidavits of fear of rescue were made, and the warrants thereupon issued, and the three fugitives were delivered over to the U.S. Marshal, and hurried off to Maryland. They were a father and his two sons, father about forty-five, and sons eighteen or nineteen. The evidence show them to have recently escaped. The father is the brother of the Rev. Dr. Pennington, a highly respected colored preacher of this city.

New York, May 28th

Last evening the church at the corner of Prince and Marion streets was filled with an intelligent audience of white and colored people, to hear Dr. Pennington relate the circumstance connected with the arrest of his brother and nephews. He showed, that he attempted to afford his brother the assistance of counsel, but was unable to do so, the officers at the Marshal's office having deceived him in relation to the time the trial was to take place before the Commissioners.

98

Hon. E. F. Culver next addressed the audience, showing, that a great injustice had been done to the brother of Dr. Pennington, and though he, up to that time, had advocated peace, he now had the spirit to tear down the building over the Marshal's head. Intense interest was manifested during the proceedings, and much sympathy in behalf of Dr. Pennington.

In the midst of the doctor's grief, friends of the slaves soon raised money to purchase his brother—about a thousand dollars; but the unfortunate sons were doomed to the auction block and the far South where not even the pen of William Still was able to reach.

Yet during this period, Still learned that his brother Peter had been able to amass the sum of money his family's captor asked. The lecture tours and fund-raising meetings his brother had arranged in the North had resulted in his raising the five thousand dollars McKiernon had demanded for his family. They were able to make contact with McKiernon, who accepted the money. And, so, finally, there was a grand reconciliation of the oldest Still child and his rescued loved ones.

chapter six

Vina, Catherine, Peter, and Levin arrived at James's house in Medford, New Jersey, on the 13th of January, 1855. Peter Still and his family accepted the invitation to stay with their freeborn relatives until a house and a piece of land could be found for them. The meeting was so joyously tearful that none could relive the blur of events leading to the scene without a great deal of disbelief at their good fortune.

Pleased that his brother's family had at last been redeemed after years of ceaseless work on the part of the distraught father, William Still turned his attention again to matters concerning the Underground Railroad. In fact, around that time, he sat in the Anti-slavery office and listened, with several members of the Vigilance Committee, to the former life in slavery of a woman named Mary Epps and two brothers, Joseph and Robert Robinson.

Mary originated in Petersburg and the Robinsons in Richmond; but their paths crossed aboard the schooner owned by a Captain Bayliss, known in Underground Railroad circles as Captain B. By offering to bring north any "freight" able to pay for space, he made himself eligible for the role of "conductor."

The risks were grave, but if the fugitive got hold of fifty or one hundred dollars, "by hook or by crook," he met the qualifications for the ride; that is, if he also found a local antislavery person to guide him to the ship.

Mary's husband longed for freedom for himself, but the thought of his wife pining away back in slavery forced him to use the hundred dollars he had saved for his own fare for her passage. Captain Bayliss promised to deliver her to the Vigilance Committee in Philadelphia; and about the 1st of March, 1855, the intrepid captain kept his word.

Still noted in his records she was about forty five years old, agreeable in manner, dark complexion, full-fleshed, and intelligent. She had been the mother of fifteen children —four of whom had been sold away from her. One remained in slavery. The others were dead.

Members of the Vigilance Committee listened to her wish that her husband could be led to safety so that she could be close to him. After receiving food and clothing she was forwarded on to Canada. When the following letter came to the office from her from Queen Victoria's land, they read it with pleasure:

Toronto, March 14th, 1855

Dear Mr. Still:—I take this opportunity of addressing you with these few lines to inform you that I have arrived here to day, and hope that this may find yourself and Mrs. Still well, as this leaves me at the present. I will also say to you, that I had no difficulty in getting along. The two young men that was with me left me at Suspension Bridge. They went another way.

I cannot say much about the place as I have ben here but a short time but so far as I have seen I like very well. You will give my Respect to your lady, & Mr and Mrs Brown. If you have not written to Petersburg you please to write as soon as can I have nothing More to Write at present but yours Respectfully

Emma Brown (old name Mary Epps)

The two fugitives who arrived with her in Philadelphia gave their names as Joseph and Robert.

Joseph was of a dark orange color, medium size, very attractive and intelligent, and was well-schooled in the art of behaving himself. He had been sold three times, and had the misfortune to fall into the hands of a cruel master each time. Sundays as well as weekdays found him bent down to labor. He had few privileges. And he had been beaten and knocked around shamefully. Therefore, he fled, leaving behind a wife and four little children. He was owned by George E. Sadler, keeper of an oyster house, and a man described as "a most heartless wretch."

His younger brother, Robert, was owned by Robert Slater, a regular slave trader. During the eight whole years Robert worked at the slave prison, his chores consisted in locking up the prison to prevent escapes, and preparing slaves for sale. Since he was a very intelligent young man, he came to know the customs and usages of the slave prison as a Pennsylvania farmer knows his barnyard stock. Therefore, he was able to furnish the Vigilance Committee in Philadelphia with details of the slave trade which were harrowing in the extreme.

To prepare slaves for market it was the custom to grease and shine the skin of black men with oil. And he stated that "females as well as males were not uncommonly stripped naked, lashed flat to a bench, and then held by two men, sometimes four, while the brutal trader would strap them with broad leather straps." The strap was preferred to the cowhide, as it would not break the skin and damage the sale. "One hundred lashes would only be a common flogging. Often I would be flogged for refusing to flog others." The separation of families would be thought nothing of.

When he reached the age of twenty-three years, Robert decided to chance running off. He approached Captain B. and asked if he would take him aboard his schooner. The seaman was about to depart with a cargo of "freight," and advised the black man he would consent to take him if he could get three passengers at a hundred dollars each.

"Very well," said Robert to the Captain, "to-day I will please my master so well, that I will catch him at an unguarded moment, and will ask him for a pass to go to a ball to-night (slave-holders love to see their slaves fiddling and dancing of nights), and as I shall be leaving in a hurry, I will take a grab from the day's sale, and when Slater hears of me again, I will be in Canada."

So after having attended to all his disagreeable duties, he made his "grab," and got a handful. That evening, instead of participating with all the dancers, he was just one degree lower than Captain B.'s deck, with several hundred dollars in his pocket, after having paid the worthy Captain one hundred each for himself and his brother, besides making the Captain a present of one hundred dollars.

The seaman was too shrewd to take out papers for Philadelphia, for they always searched vessels going there. Instead, he made it a practice to declare the destination of his ship as Washington, Baltimore, or Wilmington. Because he did not take the risk of sailing for other than a Southern port, he had a long history of successful voyages into free soil ports.

A good wind and tide took them to Philadelphia.

Shortly before their arrival, the members of the Vigilance Committee read in the Richmond *Dispatch,* an enterprising paper printed in the interest of slaveholders, an interesting column containing elegant illustrations of "runaway negroes," and stating that the unfortunate Slater had "lost fifteen hundred dollars in North Carolina money, and also his dark orange-colored, intelligent, and good-looking turnkey, Bob."

"Served him right. It is no stealing for one piece of property to go off with another piece," reasoned Still.

A few days after the notice in the *Dispatch,* the three Underground Railroad passengers arrived, and so accurate were the descriptions in the paper that the members of the Committee recognized them instantly, and without ceremony read to them the advertisement, and asked them directly: "Are you the ones?"

"We are," they owned up quickly.

The Committee did not see a dollar of the money, but understood they had about nine hundred after paying the Captain. Bob considered he "made a good grab," but did not admit that the amount advertised was correct.

After a good rest they departed for Canada. Joseph, the older brother, sent a letter back to William Still advising him of life under the "British Lion."

Saint Catharine, April 16, 1855

Mr. William Still, Dear Sir:—Your letter of date April 7th I have just got, it had been opened before it came to me. I have

104

not received any other letter from you and can get no account of them in the Post Office in this place, I am well and have got a good situation in this city and intend staying here. I should be very glad to hear from you as soon as convenient and also from all of my friends near you. My Brother is also at work with me and doing well.

There is nothing here that would interest you in the way of news. There is a Masonic Lodge of our people and two churches and societies here and some other institutions for our benefit. Be kind enough to send a few lines to the Lady spoken of for that mocking bird and much oblige me. Write me soon and believe me your obedient Servt.

Love & respects to Lady and daughter

Joseph Robinson

As well as writing to William Still, Joe and Bob had the assurance to write back to the trader and oyster-house keeper. They stated in their letter that they had arrived safely in Canada, and were having a good time. Indeed, they wrote that now they, too, enjoyed an abundance of the best—the choicest wines and brandies, which they supposed their former owners would give a great deal to have a "smack at." Then the fugitives offered to their former owners an invitation to visit them, suggesting that the quickest way for them to get to Canada would be by telegraphic wire. But in order to avail themselves of this mode of transportation, it was necessary to grease themselves thoroughly, and hang on fast! The better to slip through the wires. What gall and wormwood for the slavers!

It was a coincidence that Captain B. was in Richmond. He happened to be present when the owner of Joe read the letter at the oyster-house. Enraged, the trader told the Captain he would give "two thousand dollars if he could get them." He ranted on with an offer of "every cent they would bring, which would be over two thousand dollars, as they were 'so very likely.' "

Being good at concealing his true feelings, the Captain was never in the least suspected of having been an accomplice.

Since more and more fugitives began to arrive at the Anti-slavery office in Philadelphia, the organization became more sophisticated in accommodating them. Letters came from Hiram Wilson, the conductor in Elmira, New York, who forwarded the Canada-bound over the lake into Toronto. They came from S. H. Gay, former editor of the *Anti-Slavery Standard* and New York *Tribune* who suggested that William Still comply with the following code: "When it is possible, I wish you would advise me two days before a shipment of your intention, as Napoleon is not always on hand to look out for them at short notice. In special cases you might advise me by Telegraph, thus: 'One M. (or one F.) this morning. W. S.' By which I shall understand that one Male, or one Female, as the case may be, has left Phila. by the 6 *o'clock train*—one or more, also, as the case may be."

The Philadelphia Vigilance Committee hummed with activity. One of its duties, upon hearing of slaves brought into the state by their masters, was to inform such persons that since they were brought into the state by their owners, they were not fugitives—and as such were entitled to their freedom. This advice was a service offered by the Committee free of charge. Not only advice but assistance. The slave merely had to accept the proffered services.

Many shrewd slaveholders understood the law in this instance, and hesitated to bring their slaves onto free soil. Others, unmindful of the law, or too arrogant to heed it—such as Colonel John H. Wheeler of North Carolina, the United States Minister to Nicaragua—brought his slaves into Philadelphia.

In passing through the city from Washington one warm day in July, 1855, accompanied by three of his slaves, Colonel Wheeler came face to face with resolute members of the Vigilance Committee, in particular, William Still and Passmore Williamson.

The following letter to the New York *Tribune* bares the facts of the fracas that ensued:

Philadelphia, Monday, July 30, 1855

As the public have not been made acquainted with the facts and particulars respecting the agency of Mr. Passmore Williamson and others, in relation to the slave case now agitating this city, and especially as the poor slave mother and her two sons have been so grossly misrepresented, I deem it my duty to lay the facts before you, for publication or otherwise, as you may think proper.

On Wednesday afternoon, week, at 4½ o'clock, the following note was placed in my hands by a colored boy whom I had never before seen, to my recollection:

"Mr. Still—*Sir:* Will you come down to Bloodgood's Hotel as soon as possible—as there are three fugitive slaves here and they want liberty. Their master is here with them, on his way to New York."

The note was without date, and the signature so indistinctly written as not to be understood by me, having evidently been penned in a moment of haste.

Without delay I ran with the note to Mr. P. Williamson's office, Seventh and Arch, found him at his desk, and gave it to him, and after reading it, he remarked that he could not go down, as he had to go to Harrisburg that night on business—but he advised me to go, and get the names of the slave-

107

holder and the slaves, in order to telegraph to New York and to have them arrested there, as no time remained to procure a writ of habeas corpus here.

I could not have been two minutes in Mr. W.'s office before starting in haste for the wharf. To my surprise, however, when I reached the wharf, there I found Mr. W., his mind having undergone a sudden change; he was soon on the spot.

I saw three or four colored persons in the hall at Bloodgood's, none of whom I recognized except the boy who brought me the note. Before having time for making inquiry some one said they had gone on board the boat. "Get their description," said Mr. W. I instantly inquired of one of the colored persons for the desired description, and was told that she was "a tall, dark woman, with two little boys."

Mr. W. and myself ran on board of the boat, looked among the passengers on the first deck, but saw them not. "They are up on the second deck," an unknown voice uttered. In a second we were in their presence. We approached the anxious-looking slave-mother with her two boys on her left-hand; close on her right sat an ill-favored white man having a cane in his hand which I took to be a sword-cane. (As to its being a sword-cane, however, I might have been mistaken.)

The first words to the mother were: "Are you traveling?"

"Yes," was the prompt answer.

"With whom?"

She nodded her head toward the ill-favored man, signifying with him. Fidgeting on his seat, he said something, exactly what I do not now recollect. In reply I remarked: "Do they belong to you, Sir?"

"Yes, they are in my charge," was his answer. Turning from him to the mother and her sons, in substance, and word for word, as near as I can remember, the following remarks were earnestly though calmly addressed by the individuals

108

who rejoiced to meet them on free soil, and who felt unmistakably assured that they were justified by the laws of Pennsylvania as well as the Law of the Lord, in informing them of their rights:

"You are entitled to your freedom according to the laws of Pennsylvania, having been brought into the State by your owner. If you prefer freedom to slavery, and we suppose everybody does, you have the chance to accept it now. Act calmly—don't be frightened by your master—you are as much entitled to your freedom as we are, or as he is—be determined and you need have no fears but that you will be protected by the law. Judges have time and again decided cases in this city and State similar to yours in favor of freedom! Of course, if you want to remain a slave with your master, we cannot force you to leave; we only want to make you sensible of your rights. *Remember, if you lose this chance you may never get such another,"* etc.

This advice to the woman was made in the hearing of a number of persons present, white and colored; and one elderly white gentleman of genteel address, who seemed to take much interest in what was going on, remarked that they would have the same chance for their freedom in New Jersey and New York, as they then had—seeming to sympathize with the woman, etc.

During the few moments in which the above remarks were made, the slave-holder frequently interrupted—said she understood all about the laws making her free, and her right to leave if she wanted to; but contended that she did not want to leave—that she was on a visit to New York to see her friends—afterward *wished to return to her three children whom she left in Virginia, from whom it would be* HARD *to separate her.* Furthermore, he diligently tried to constrain her to say that she did not want to be interfered with—that she wanted to go with him—that she was on a visit to New York—had children in the South, etc.; but the woman's de-

109

sire to be free was altogether too strong to allow her to make a single acknowledgment favorable to his wishes in the matter. On the contrary, she repeatedly said, distinctly and firmly, *"I am not free, but I want my freedom*—ALWAYS *wanted to be free!! but he holds me."*

While the slave-holder claimed that she belonged to him, he said *that she was free!* Again he said that he was *going to give her her freedom,* etc. When his eyes would be off hers, such eagerness as her looks expressed, indicative of her entreaty that we would not forsake her and her little ones in their weakness, it had never been my lot to witness before, under any circumstances.

The last bell tolled! The last moment for further delay passed! The arm of the woman being slightly touched, accompanied with the word, "Come!" she instantly arose. "Go along—go along!" said some, who sympathized, to the boys, at the same time taking hold of their arms. By this time the parties were fairly moving toward the stairway leading to the deck below. Instantly on their starting, the slave-holder rushed at the woman and her children, to prevent their leaving; and, if I am not mistaken, he simultaneously took hold of the woman and Mr. Williamson, which resistance on his part caused Mr. W. to take hold of him and set him aside quickly.

The passengers were looking on all around, but none interfered in behalf of the slave-holder except one man, whom I took to be another slave-holder. He said harshly, "Let them alone; they are his *property!"* The youngest boy, about 7 years of age—too young to know what these things meant—cried "Massa John! Massa John!" The elder boy, 11 years of age, took the matter more dispassionately, and the mother *quite calmly.* The mother and her sympathizers all moved down the stairs together in the presence of quite a number of spectators on the first deck and on the wharf, all of whom, as far as I was able to discern, seemed to look upon the whole

110

affair with the greatest indifference. The woman and children were assisted, but not forced to leave. Nor were there any violence or threatenings as I saw or heard. The only words that I heard from any one of an objectionable character, were: "Knock him down; knock him down!" but who uttered it or who was meant I knew not, nor have I since been informed. However, if it was uttered by a colored man, I regret it, as there was not the slightest cause for such language, especially as the sympathies of the spectators and citizens seemed to justify the course pursued.

While passing off the wharf and down Delaware-avenue to Dock st., and up Dock to Front, where a carriage was procured, the slave-holder and one police officer were of the party, if no more.

The youngest boy on being put in the carriage was told that he was "a fool for crying so after 'Massa John,' who would sell him if he ever caught him." Not another whine was heard on the subject.

The carriage drove down town slowly, the horses being fatigued and the weather intensely hot; the inmates were put out on Tenth street—not at any house—after which they soon found hospitable friends and quietude. The excitement of the moment having passed by, the mother *seemed very cheerful, and rejoiced greatly that herself and boys had been, as she thought, so "providentially delivered from the house of bondage!"* For the first time in her life she could look upon herself and children and feel free!

Having felt the iron in her heart for the best half of her days—having been sold with her children on the auction block—having had one of her children sold far away from her without hope of her seeing him again—she very naturally and wisely concluded to go to Canada, fearing if she remained in this city—as some assured her she could do with entire safety—that she might again find herself in the clutches of the tyrant from whom she had fled.

111

A few items of what she had related concerning the character of her master may be interesting to the reader—

Within the last two years he had sold all his slaves—between thirty and forty in number—having purchased the present ones in that space of time. She said that before leaving Washington, coming on the cars, and at his father-in-law's in this city, a number of persons had told him that in bringing his slaves into Pennsylvania they would be free. When told at his father-in-law's, as she overheard it, that he "could not have done a worse thing," &c., he replied that "Jane would not leave him."

As much, however, as he affected to have such implicit confidence in Jane, he scarcely allowed her to be out of his presence a moment while in this city. To use Jane's own language, he was "on her heels every minute," fearing that some one might get to her ears the sweet music of freedom. By the way, Jane had it deep in her heart before leaving the South, and was bent on succeeding in New York, if disappointed in Philadelphia.

At Bloodgood's, after having been belated and left by the 2 o'clock train, while waiting for the 5 o'clock line, his appetite tempted her "master" to take a hasty dinner. So after placing Jane where he thought she would be pretty secure from "evil communications" from the colored waiters, and after giving her a double counselling, he made his way to the table; remained but a little while, however, before leaving to look after Jane; finding her composed, looking over a banister near where he left her, he returned to the table again and finished his meal.

But alas for the slave-holder! Jane had her "top eye open," and in that brief space had appealed to the sympathies of a person whom she ventured to trust, saying, "I and my children are slaves and we want liberty!" I am not certain, but suppose that person, in the goodness of his heart, was the cause of the note being sent to the Anti-slavery office, and hence the result.

As to her going on to New York to see her friends, and wishing to return to her three children in the South, and his going to free her, &c., Jane declared repeatedly and very positively, that there was not a particle of truth in what her master said on these points. The truth is she had not the slightest hope of freedom through any act of his. She had only left one boy in the South, who had been sold far away, where she scarcely ever heard from him, indeed never expected to see him any more.

In appearance Jane is tall and well formed, high and large forehead, of genteel manners, chestnut color, and seems to possess, naturally, uncommon good sense, though of course she has never been allowed to read.

Thus I have given as truthful a report as I am capable of doing, of Jane and the circumstances connected with her deliverance.

W. Still

Colonel Wheeler was determined not to let Jane and the boys go without a fight. He swore before a Committing Magistrate in Philadelphia that his slaves had been abducted forcibly by William Still, Passmore Williamson, and five other colored men. The officials brought them to trial, for "assault and battery" in the case of Williamson, "forcible abduction" on the part of Still, and "riot" on the parts of the five others who happened to be on the scene.

An agitated feeling developed throughout the city. But the members of the Vigilance Committee stood firm. Passmore Williamson, who was the first to be tried, denied any knowledge of the whereabouts of Jane and the boys, stating

113

that he had left the city upon prior business immediately after the incident and that, upon his return, had inquired merely after their safety, not wishing to be in the position of having either to perjure himself or incriminate others.

Williamson suffered an examination from Judge Kane which might have broken the spirit of a lesser man. But in doing so, he won the admiration and sympathy of the friends of humanity and liberty throughout the country. In the end, as proof of his fidelity, he submitted cheerfully to imprisonment, on the flimsy pretext of "contempt of court," rather than desert his principles.

At first, the trial seemed to the proslavery element an opportunity for teaching abolitionists and blacks not to interfere with a "chivalrous Southern gentleman" while passing through the North with his slaves. But they had not anticipated that Williamson's firm stand would bring sympathy from the ablest and best minds throughout the North. The affair catalyzed a rapidly awakening interest in abolition among thousands who had hitherto shown little or no interest at all on the wrongs done to slaves.

The proslavery element realized that keeping Mr. Williamson in prison was indirectly aiding the cause of freedom. Every day he remained behind bars brought more converts to the cause of liberty. Indeed, he was doing more for the cause of liberty in prison than he could possibly have accomplished while pursuing his ordinary vocation.

Regarding the others under bonds, Colonel Wheeler and his friends felt confident they would not escape punishment either. They were brought into court for trial, while Passmore Williamson sat in prison receiving visits from hosts of friends.

The case against William Still was next. The friends of the slave expected all manner of accusations and false swearing against him. James McKim, prepared for the onslaught, engaged the Honorable Charles Gibbons to defend him— with William Pierce and William Birney to defend the five other defendants.

James McKim and the lawyers for the defense, desiring to make the victory complete, decided to have Jane Johnson present in the courtroom in order to face her master and destroy his "refuge of lies." Therefore, she was brought out at the opening of the defense. With Mrs. McKim, Lucretia Mott, and several other antislavery women sitting by her side, Jane faced her master boldly. She prepared to contradict all that he had sworn under oath.

Lifting the heavy veil which disguised her from the crowd outside the courthouse, she answered the call, "Jane Johnson . . . take the stand!" The scene was indescribably dramatic. In a shrill voice, she testified bravely. Her testimony was in keeping with the following affadavit:

State of New York, City and County of New York.

Jane Johnson, being sworn, makes oath and says—
My name is Jane—Jane Johnson; I was the slave of Mr. Wheeler of Washington. He bought me and my two children, about two years ago, of Mr. Cornelius Crew, of Richmond, Va.; my youngest child is between six and seven years old, the other between ten and eleven; I have one other child only, and he is in Richmond; I have not seen him for about two years; never expect to see him again; Mr. Wheeler brought me and my two children to Philadelphia, on the way to Nicaragua, to wait on his wife; I didn't want to go without my two children, and he consented to take them; we came to Philadelphia by the cars; stopped at Mr. Sully's, Mr. Wheeler's father-in-law, a few moments; then went to the steamboat for New York at 2 o'clock, but were too late; we went into Bloodgood's Hotel; Mr. Wheeler went to dinner; Mr. Wheeler

115

had told me in Washington to have nothing to say to colored persons, and if any of them spoke to me, to say I was a free woman traveling with a minister; we staid at Bloodgood's till 5 o'clock; Mr. Wheeler kept his eye on me all the time except when he was at dinner; he left his dinner to come and see if I was safe, and then went back again; while he was at dinner, I saw a colored woman and told her I was a slave woman, that my master had told me not to speak to colored people, and that if any of them spoke to me to say that I was free; but I am not free; but I want to be free; she said, "poor thing, I pity you;" after that I saw a colored man and said the same thing to him, he said he would telegraph to New York, and two men would meet me at 9 o'clock and take me with them; after that we went on board the boat, Mr. Wheeler sat beside me on the deck; I saw a colored gentleman come on board, he beckoned to me. I nodded my head, and could not go; Mr. Wheeler was beside me and I was afraid; a white gentleman [Jane took Passmore Williamson to be white] then came and said to Mr. Wheeler, "I want to speak to your servant, and tell her of her rights;" Mr. Wheeler rose and said, "If you have anything to say, say it to me— she knows her rights;" the white gentleman asked me if I wanted to be free; I said "I do, but I belong to this gentleman and I can't have it;" he replied, "Yes, you can, come with us, you are as free as your master, if you want your freedom come now; if you go back to Washington you may never get it;" I rose to go, Mr. Wheeler spoke, and said, "I will give you your freedom," but he had never promised it before, and I knew he would never give it to me; the white gentleman held out his hand and I went toward him; I was ready for the word before it was given me; I took the children by the hands, who both cried, for they were frightened, but both stopped when they got on shore; a colored man carried the little one, I led the other by the hand. We walked down

116

the street till we got to a hack; nobody forced me away; nobody pulled me, and nobody led me; I went away of my own free will; I always wished to be free and meant to be free when I came North; I hardly expected it in Philadelphia, but I thought I should get free in New York; I have been comfortable and happy since I left Mr. Wheeler, and so are the children; I don't want to go back; I could have gone in Philadelphia if I had wanted to; I could go now; but I had rather die than go back. I wish to make this statement before a magistrate, because I understand that Mr. Williamson is in prison on my account, and I hope the truth may be of benefit to him.

her

Jane ✕ Johnson

mark

It might be supposed that her honest and straightforward testimony would have been sufficient to cause Wheeler to abandon his pursuit. But he hung on to his "lost cause" tenaciously. And his counsel, David Webster, and the United States District Attorney, Vandyke, completely imbued with the proslavery spirit, were equally unyielding. And so, with a zeal befitting the most worthy object imaginable, they labored with untiring effort to obtain a conviction.

By this policy, however, the counsel for the defense was doubly aroused. Mr. Gibbons perfectly annihilated the "distinguished Colonel John H. Wheeler, United States Minister Plenipotentiary near the Island of Nicaragua," taking special pains to ring the changes repeatedly on his long appellations. Indeed, Mr. Gibbons was forcible and eloquent on whatever point of law he chose to touch or in whatever

117

direction he chose to glance at the injustice and cruelty of the South. Vividly, he drew the contrast between the states of Georgia and Pennsylvania, with regard to the atrocious laws of Georgia.

With the District Attorney, William B. Mann (whose sentiments were antislavery), and his Honor, Judge Kelley, the defendants had no cause to complain. Throughout the entire proceedings, they had reason to believe that neither of these officials sympathized in the least with Wheeler or slavery. Indeed, in the Judge's charge, and also in the District Attorney's closing speech, the ring of freedom could be distinctly heard—much more so than was agreeable to Wheeler and his proslavery sympathizers.

William Still's case ended in his acquittal for lack of evidence; that of the five other colored men was then taken up.

At the conclusion of the trial, the jury returned a verdict of "not guilty," as to all the persons, in the first count, charging them with riot. In the second count, charging them with "assault and battery," Ballard and Curtis were found "guilty," the rest "not guilty." The guilty were given about a week in jail.

The following extract, taken from the correspondence of the New York *Tribune,* touches Jane Johnson's presence in the court.

. . . it was a bold and perilous move on the part of her friends, and the deepest apprehensions were felt for a while, for the result. The United States Marshal was there with his warrant and an extra force to execute it. The officers of the court and other State officers were there to protect the witness and vindicate the laws of the State. Vandyke, the United States District Attorney, swore he would take her. The State officers swore he should not, and for a while it seemed that nothing could avert a bloody scene. It was suspected

118

that the conflict would take place at the door, when she should leave the room, so that when she and her friends went out, and for some time after, the most intense suspense pervaded the court-room. She was, however, allowed to enter the carriage that awaited her without disturbance. She was accompanied by Mr. McKim, Secretary of the Pennsylvania Anti-Slavery Society, Lucretia Mott and George Corson, one of our most manly and intrepid police officers. The carriage was followed by another filled with officers as a guard; and thus escorted she was taken back in safety to the house from which she had been brought. . . .

Passmore Williamson began his sentence on the 27th day of July, 1855. He was released on the 3rd of November. By doing so, he gained, in the estimation of the friends of freedom everywhere, a triumph and a fame which few men in the great moral battle of the time could claim.

Letters poured into the Committee from every corner of the antislavery world. All heaped praise on Williamson for his bravery. This one, from Reverend N. R. Johnston, who in earlier days had commiserated with Still on Seth Concklin's fate, drew William Still's close attention:

Topsham, Vt., September 1st, 1855

Wm. Still, my dear Friend:—I have the heart, but not the time, to write you a long letter. It is Saturday evening, and I am preparing to preach to-morrow afternoon from Heb. xiii. 3, "Remember them that are in bonds as bound with them." This will be my second sermon from this text. Sabbath before last I preached from it, arguing and illustrating the proposition, deduced from it, that "the great work to which we are now called is the abolition of Slavery, or the emancipation of the slave," showing our duty as *philanthropists*. To-morrow I intend to point out our duty as *citi-*

zens. Some to whom I minister, I know, will call it a political speech; but I have long since determined to speak for the dumb what is in my heart and in my Bible, let men hear or forbear. I am accountable to the God of the oppressed, not to man. If I have his favor, why need I regard man's disfavor? Many besides the members of my own church come out regularly to hear me. Some of them are pro-slavery politicians. The consequence is, I preach much on the subject of Slavery. And while I have a tongue to speak, and lips to pray, they shall never be sealed or silent so long as millions of dumb have so few to speak for them.

But poor Passmore Williamson is in bonds. Let us also remember him, as bound with him. He has many sympathizers. I am glad you did not share the same fate. For some reasons I am sorry you have fallen into the hands of thieves. For some others I am glad. It will make you more devoted to your good work. Persecution always brightens the Christian, and gives more zeal to the true philanthropist. I hope you will come off victorious. I pray for you and your co-laborers and co-sufferers.

My good brother, I am greatly indebted to you for your continued kindness. The Lord reward you.

I have a scholarship in an Ohio College, Geneva Hall, which will entitle me—any one I may send—to six years tuition. It is an Anti-slavery institution, and wholly under Anti-slavery control and influence. They want colored students to prepare them for the great field of labor open to men of talent and piety of that class. When I last saw you I purposed talking to you about this matter, but was disappointed very much in not getting to take tea with you, as I partly promised. Have you a son ready for college? or for the grammar school? Do you know any promising young man who would accept my scholarship? Or would your brother's son, Peter or Levin, like to have the benefit of it? If so, you are at liberty to promise it to any one whom you think I would be willing to educate. Write me at your earliest convenience, about this matter. . . .

I presume the *Standard* will contain full accounts of the Norristown meeting, the Williamson case, and your own and those connected. If it does not, I will thank you to write me fully.

What causes the delay of that book, the History of Peter Still's family, etc.? I long to see it.

The Lord bless you in your labors for the slave. Yours, etc.,

N. R. Johnston

That Peter Still's tragic life was to be made the subject of a book by Mrs. Kate Pickard was well known throughout abolitionist circles. Its publication, eagerly awaited, coincided with the collection of funds which Peter had amassed for their rescue. The title of the book, *The Kidnapped and the Ransomed,* seemed apropos.

But to expect the boys, Peter or Levin—deprived of the rudiments of reading and writing in their life of slavery—to be prepared to enter a college was preposterous. It was incredible enough that they had escaped with all their faculties intact. Caroline, William Still's own daughter, was too young to take advantage of the opportunity at the time.

Word also came from Abigail Goodwin, whose devotion to the cause of the slave equaled that of her friend, Lucretia Mott.

September 9, 1855
Salem, New Jersey

Dear Friend:—I am truly rejoiced and thankful that the right has triumphed. But stranger had it been otherwise, in your intelligent community, where it must be apparent to all who inquire into it, that you had done nothing but what was deserving of high commendation, instead of blame and punishment; and shame on the jury who would bring in the two men guilty of assault and battery. They ought to have another trial; perhaps another jury would be more just. It is well for the credit of Philadelphia, that there is one upright judge, as Kelley seems to be, and his sentence will be a light one it is presumed, showing he considered the charge a mere pretence.

I hope and trust, that neither thyself nor the other men will have much if any expense to bear; your lawyers will not charge anything I suppose, and the good citizens will pay all else. It seems there are hopes entertained that Passmore Williamson will soon be set at liberty It must be a great comfort to him and wife, in their trials, that it will conduce to the furtherance of the good cause.

If Philadelphians are not aroused now after this great stretch of power, to consider their safety, they must be a stupid set of people, but it must certainly do good. . . . You will take good care of Jane Johnson, I hope, and not let her get kidnapped back to Slavery. Is it safe for her to remain in your city or anywhere else in our "free land?" I have some doubts and fears for her; do try to impress her with the necessity of being very cautious and careful against deceivers, pretended friends. She had better be off to Canada pretty soon.

Thy wife must not sit up washing and ironing all night again. She ought to have help in her sympathy and labors for the poor fugitives, and, I should think there are many who would willingly assist her.

I intended to be careful of trespassing upon thy time, as thee must have enough to do; the fugitives are still coming I expect. With kind regards, also to thy wife, your friend,

A. Goodwin

After more thought, Abigail sent another note to Still.

122

Would it not be well to get up a committee of women, to provide clothes for fugitive females—a dozen women sewing a day, or even half a day of each week, might keep a supply always ready, they might, I should think, get the merchants or some of them, to give cheap materials—mention it to thy wife, and see if she cannot get up a society. I will do what I can here for it. I enclose five dollars for the use of fugitives. It was a good while that I heard nothing of your rail road concern; I expected thee had gone to Canada, or has the journey not been made, or is it yet to be accomplished, or given up? I was in hopes thee would go and see with thy own eyes how things go on in that region of fugitives, and if it's a goodly land to live in. . . .

William Still made plans to visit the various fugitive slave settlements in Canada such as the "Buxton" and the "Elgin" communities. Some of his colleagues questioned the work habits of the fugitives as well as their life-style. Never, for a moment, had Still doubted the industry, cleanliness, and thrift that the many runaways who had passed through his station in Philadelphia would display in the new land. As a general rule, only the most energetic, intelligent, and industrious slaves took the risks of running off.

To dispel the rumors, Still undertook the long journey into Canada. After a thorough tour of the various "settlements" he returned to Philadelphia convinced that the colored people who had migrated there were above the average in the qualities that go to make good citizens. He had the word, in the vast majority of instances, of their landlords and employers to back his evidence.

Once home, the Underground Railroad flourished, as never before.

chapter seven

Days as well as nights found Still busy fulfilling the obligations of his appointment as Chairman of the Acting Committee. Not only did he work to raise funds to care for the needs of the rapidly increasing number of fugitives, but he also kept records of all the affairs of the office, including an account of all expenditures. With the money the members of the Vigilance Committee collected, they were able to board runaway slaves for a period of a few days to as long as thirteen. Still arranged for lodgings for the fugitive and obtained clothing, medicine, and money as the case warranted.

Few Committee men equaled the devotion shown by him. It was a common occurrence for Still to leave his supper table in the middle of a meal to tend to the needs of a new arrival. Or a party of arrivals, as became increasingly common. Indeed, as many as five to ten or even twenty slaves took off together for the freedom of the North. And the mode of transportation ranged from foot travel to horse and wagon "borrowed" from their masters, to a sea voyage aboard an Underground Railroad schooner under one of several daring sea captains such as Captain Bayliss.

124

Whenever one of these captains arrived in Philadelphia with a cargo of fugitives, William Still marveled that they as white men broke the laws of their state so willingly. Helping the runaways exposed the captains to the penitentiary.

All these happenings brought zest to Still's work at the Anti-slavery office, and the modus operandi of his organization shifted constantly.

A matter was brought to Still's attention by a series of letters from a lawyer named Bigelow, who lived and worked for the Underground Railroad in Washington, D.C. For the past several years he had corresponded with the office in Philadelphia about fugitives who came through his station, but this time he persisted in a matter of more than passing interest to him:

Washington, D.C., September 9th, 1855

Mr. William Still, Dear Sir:—I strongly hope the little matter of business so long pending and about which I have written you so many times, will take a move now. I have the promise that the merchandise shall be delivered in this city to-night. Like so many other promises, this also may prove a failure, though I have reason to believe that it will not. I shall, however, know before I mail this note. In case the goods arrive here I shall hope to see your long-talked of "Professional gentleman" in Washington, as soon as possible. He will find me by the enclosed card, which shall be a satisfactory introduction for him. You have never given me his name, nor am I anxious to know it. But on the pleasant visit made last fall to friend Wm. Wright, in Adams Co., I suppose I accidentally learned it to be a certain Dr. H—. Well, let him come.

I had an interesting call a week ago from two gentlemen, masters of vessels, and brothers, one of whom, I understand, you know as the "powder boy." [Here he refers to a sea captain who had been engaged at different times in carrying powder in his boat from a powder magazine, and had, thereby, received the name.] I had a little light freight for them; but not finding enough other freight to ballast their craft, they went down the river looking for wheat, and promising to return soon. I hope to see them often.

I hope this may find you returned from your northern trip, as your time proposed was out two or three days ago.

I hope if the whole particulars of Jane Johnson's case are printed, you will send me the copy as proposed.

I forwarded some of her things to Boston a few days ago, and had I known its importance in court, I could have sent you one or two witnesses who would prove that her freedom was intended by her before she left Washington, and that a man was *engaged* here to go on to Philadelphia the same day with her to give notice there of her case, though I think he failed to do so. It was beyond all question her purpose, *before leaving Washington and provable too,* that if Wheeler should make her a free woman by taking her to a free state, *"to use it rather."*

Tuesday, 11th September. The attempt was made on Sunday to forward the merchandise, but failed through no fault of any of the parties that I know of. It will be repeated soon, and you shall know the result.

"Whorra for Judge Kane." I feel so indignant at the man, that it is not easy to write the foregoing sentence, and yet who is helping our cause like Kane and Douglass, not forgetting Stringfellow. I hope soon to know that this reaches you in safety.

It often happens that light freight would be offered to Captain B., but the owners cannot by possibility *advance* the amount of freight. I wish it were possible in some such extreme cases, that after advancing *all they have,* some public fund should be found to pay the balance, or at least lend it.

[I wish here to caution you against the supposition that I would do any act, or say a word towards helping servants to escape. Although I hate slavery so much, I keep my hands clear of any such wicked or illegal act.] Yours, very truly,

J. B.

Will you recollect, hereafter, that in any of my future letters, in which I may use [   ] whatever words may be within the brackets are intended to have no signification whatever to you, only to blind the eyes of the uninitiated. You will find an example at the close of my letter.

Of course it was the business of the Vigilance Committee, which was clearly understood by all the friends of the slave, to assist the needy fugitive who managed to reach them in Philadelphia. But it was not an organization which sent agents south to incite slaves to run away or to assist them in so doing. But like many another rule, this was difficult to adhere to. Who had the heart to turn a deaf ear to the cries of the suffering?

What the signer "J.B." refers to is indicated by some earlier correspondence dealing in this particular case: a young slave girl, whose situation reveals the incessant care, anxiety, hazards, and strategy which had to be used by the antislavery men before the end result was achieved.

One of the earliest letters reads:

Washington, D. C., June 22d, 1854

Mr. William Still:—*Sir*—I have just received a letter from my friend, Wm. Wright, of York Sulphur Springs, Pa., in which he says, that by writing to you, I may get some in-

127

formation about the transportation of some *property* from this neighborhood to your city or vicinity.

A person who signs himself Wm. Penn, lately wrote to Mr. Wright, saying he would pay $300 to have this service performed. It is for the conveyance of *only one* SMALL package; but it has been discovered since, that the removal cannot be so safely affected without taking *two larger* packages with it. I understand that the *three* are to be brought to this city and stored in safety, as soon as the forwarding merchant in Philadelphia shall say he is ready to send on. The storage, etc., here, will cost a trifle, but the $300 will be promptly paid for the whole service. I think Mr. Wright's daughter, Hannah, has also seen you. I am also known to Prof. C. D. Cleveland, of your own city. If you answer this promptly, you will soon hear from Wm. Penn himself.

Very truly yours,
J. Bigelow

William Wright, one of the most devoted antislavery men in Pennsylvania, kept a station at York. It was one of the busiest ones on the Underground Railroad because it was located near the foot of the southern slope of the South Mountain—a spur of the Alleghenies extending under various names to Chattanooga, Tennessee. At first a trickle, and then a steady stream of fugitives followed this mountain in its course until they reached Wright's house.

With men such as these, William Still held high hopes for the success of the mission. He replied to Mr. Bigelow's letter and received an answer shortly afterward.

Washington, D. C., June 27, 1854

Mr. Wm. Still—*Dear Sir:*—I have to thank you for the prompt answer you had the kindness to give my note of the 22d inst. Having found a correspondence so quick and

128

easy, and withal so very flattering, I address you again more fully.

The liberal appropriation for *transportation* has been made chiefly on account of a female child of ten or eleven years old, for whose purchase I have been authorized to offer $700 (refused), and for whose sister I have paid $1,600, and some $1,000 for their mother, &c.

This child sleeps in the same apartment with its master and mistress, which adds to the difficulty of removal. She is some ten or twelve miles from the city, so that really the chief hazard will be in bringing her safely to town, and in secreting her until a few days of *storm* shall have abated. All this, I think, is now provided for with entire safety.

The child has two cousins in the immediate vicinity; a young man of some twenty-two years of age, and his sister, of perhaps seventeen—*both Slaves,* but bright and clear-headed as anybody. The young man I have seen often—the services of *both* seem indispensable to the main object suggested; but having once rendered the service, they cannot, and ought not return to Slavery. They look for *freedom* as the reward of what they shall now do.

Out of the $300, cheerfully offered for the whole enterprise, I must pay some reasonable sum for transportation to the city and sustenance while here. It cannot be much; for the balance, I shall give a draft, which will be *promptly paid* on their arrival in New York.

If I have been understood to offer the whole $300, *it shall be paid,* though I have meant as above stated. Among the various ways that have been suggested, has been that of taking *all of them* into the cars here; that, I think, will be found impracticable. I find so much vigilance at the depot, that I would not deem it safe, though in any kind of carriage they might leave in safety at any time.

All the rest I leave to the experience and sagacity of the gentleman who maps out the enterprise.

129

Now I will thank you to reply to this and let me know that it reaches you in safety, and is not put in a careless place, whereby I may be endangered; and state also, whether all my propositions are understood and acceptable, and whether, (pretty quickly after I shall inform you that *all things are ready*), the gentleman will make his appearance?

I live alone. My office and bed-room, &c., are at the corner of E. and 7th streets, opposite the east end of the General Post Office, where any one may call upon me.

It would, of course, be imprudent, that this letter, or any other *written* particulars, be in his pockets for fear of accident.

Yours very respectfully,
J. Bigelow

Up to this time the chances seemed favorable for procuring the services of either of the two sea captains who visited Bigelow for the removal of the merchandise to Philadelphia, provided the person shipping the "merchandise" had it ready to suit their convenience. But since both of these captains had many engagements in Richmond and Petersburg, Virginia, which occupied their time, the matter of expediting—or arranging for the shipment to be delivered—was laid before two professional gentlemen who held chairs at one of the medical colleges in Philadelphia. They were known to be friends of the slave and were wise in the methods of the operation of the Underground Railroad. Either of these professors would gladly have undertaken the task provided arrangements could be completed in time to be carried out during their vacation. The undertaking stayed in this promising but indefinite stage for more than a year.

During this interval, correspondence and anxiety increased. The difficulties and disappointments mounted. The hope of freedom, buoyed up in the heart of the young slave girl during the long, anxious months of waiting for the hour of deliverance, began to fade. But true and faithful, Mr. Bigelow did not abandon his promise to her.

He wrote to William Still of the state of his project in the following letter:

Washington, D. C. October 6th, 1855

Mr. Still, Dear Sir:—I regret exceedingly to learn by your favor of 4th instant, that all things are not ready. Although I cannot speak of any immediate and positive danger. [*Yet it is well known that the city is full of incendiaries.*]

Perhaps you are aware that any colored citizen is liable at any hour of day or night without any show of authority to have his house ransacked by constables, and if others do it and commit the most outrageous depredations none but white witnesses can convict them. Such outrages are always common here, and no kind of property exposed to colored protection only, can be considered safe. [I don't say that *much liberty* should not be given to constables on account of numerous runaways, but it doesn't always work for good.] Before advertising they go round and offer rewards to sharp colored men of perhaps *one or two hundred dollars,* to betray runaways, and having discovered their hiding-place, *seize* them and then cheat their informers out of the money.

[*Although a law abiding man,*] I am anxious in the case of *innocence* to raise no conflict or suspicion. [*Be sure that the manumission is full and legal.*] And as I am *powerless* without your aid, *I pray you don't* lose a moment in giving me relief. The idea of waiting yet for weeks seems dreadful; do reduce it to days if possible, and give me notice of the *earliest possible time.*

The property is not yet advertised, but will be, [and if we delay too long, may be sold and lost.]

131

It was a great misunderstanding, though not your fault, that so much delay would be necessary. [I repeat again that I must have the thing done legally, therefore, please get a good lawyer to draw up the manumission.]

Yours truly,
J. Bigelow

Great anxiety was felt in Washington. An equal amount existed in Philadelphia respecting the safety of the enterprise.

And at this stage, Mr. Bigelow decided to use the name of the renowned Quaker, William Penn, because he no longer felt it safe to write over his own name.

Washington, D. C., November 10th, 1855

Dear Sir:—Doctor T. presented my card last night about half past eight which I instantly recognized. I, however, soon became suspicious, and afterwards confounded, to find the doctor using your name and the well known names of Mr. McK. and Mr. W. and yet, neither he nor I, could conjecture the object of his visit.

The doctor is agreeable and sensible, and doubtless a true-hearted man. He seemed to see the whole matter as I did, and was embarrassed. He had nothing to propose, no information to give of the "P. Boy," or of any substitute, and seemed to want no particular information from me concerning my anxieties and perils, though I stated them to him, but found him as powerless as myself to give me relief. I had an agreeable interview with the doctor till after ten, when he left, intending to take the cars at six, as I suppose he did so, this morning.

This morning after eight, I got your letter of the 9th, but it gives me but little enlightenment or satisfaction. You simply say that the doctor is a *true man,* which I cannot doubt, that you thought it best we should have an interview, and that you supposed I would meet the expenses. You informed me also that the "P. Boy" left for Richmond, on Friday, the 2d, to be gone *the length of time named in your last,* I must infer that to be *ten days* though in your last *you assured me* that the "P. Boy" would certainly start for *this place* (not Richmond) in two or three days, though the difficulty about freight might cause delay, and the whole enterprise might not be accomplished under ten days, &c., &c. That time having elapsed and I having agreed to an extra fifty dollars to ensure promptness. I have scarcely left my office since, except for my hasty meals, awaiting his arrival. You now inform me he has gone to Richmond, to be gone ten days, which will expire to-morrow, but you do not say he will return here or to Phila., or where, at the expiration of that time, and Dr. T could tell me nothing whatever about him. Had he been able to tell me that this *best plan,* which I have so long rested upon, would fail, or was abandoned, I could then understand it, but he says no such thing, and you say, as you have twice before said, "ten days more."

Now, my dear sir, after this recapitulation, can you not see that I have reason for great embarrassment? I have given assurances, both here and in New York, founded on your assurances to me, and caused my friends in the latter place great anxiety, so much that I have had no way to explain my own letters but by sending your last two to Mr. Tappan.

I cannot doubt, I do not, but that you wish to help me, and the cause too, for which both of us have made many and large sacrifices with no hope of reward in this world. If in this case, I have been very urgent since September Dr. T. can give you some of my reasons, they have not been selfish.

The whole matter is in a nutshell. Can I, in your opinion, depend on the "P. Boy," and when?

If he promises to come here next trip, will he come, or

go to Richmond? This I think is the best way. Can I depend on it?

Dr. T. promised to write me some explanation and give some advice, and at first I thought to await his letter, but on second thought concluded to tell you how I feel, as I have done.

Will you answer my questions with some explicitness, and without delay?

I forgot to inquire of Dr. T. who is the head of your Vigilance Committee, whom I may address concerning other and further operations?

Yours very truly,
Wm. Penn

P. S. I ought to say, that I have no doubt but there were good reasons for the P. Boy's going to Richmond instead of W.; *but what can they be?*

This letter, and several which followed, shows the perplexities and dangers which often accompanied an Underground Railroad transaction. But the picture was soon to become much brighter, as was often the case in matters such as these.

In the following letter, the girl has been taken from her master:

WASHINGTON, D.C., OCTOBER 12, 1855

MR. WM. STILL:——AS YOU PICK UP ALL THE NEWS THAT IS STIRRING, I CONTRIBUTE A FEW SCRAPS TO YOUR STOCK, GOING TO SHOW THAT THE POOR SLAVE-HOLDERS HAVE THEIR TROUBLES AS WELL AS OTHER PEOPLE.

FOUR HEAVY LOSSES ON ONE SMALL SCRAP CUT FROM A SINGLE NUMBER OF THE "SUN!" HOW VEXATIOUS! HOW PROVOKING! ON THE OTHER HAND, THINK OF THE POOR, TIMID,

134

BREATHLESS, FLYING CHILD OF FIFTEEN! FIVE HUNDRED DOLLARS REWARD! OH, FOR SUCCOR! TO WHOM IN ALL THIS WIDE LAND OF FREEDOM SHALL SHE FLEE AND FIND SAFETY? ALAS!—ALAS!—THE LAW POINTS TO NO ONE!

IS SHE STILL RUNNING WITH BLEEDING FEET? OR HIDES SHE IN SOME OLD CAVE, TO REST AND STARVE? "$500 RE-WARD." YOURS FOR THE WEAK AND THE POOR. PERISH THE REWARD.

J. B.

Having succeeded in getting possession of, and secreting this fleeing girl of fifteen as best they could in Washington, all concerned were compelled to "possess their souls in patience," until the storm had passed. And since no opportunity had presented itself to prepare the "package" for shipment from Washington, neither the "powder boy" nor Dr. T. was prepared to attend the removal at this critical moment. Indeed, the other professional gentleman (Dr. H.) was now appealed to, but his engagements in the college forbade his absence until about Thanksgiving recess, which was, at that time, about six weeks off. This information was communicated to Washington, which lent the perfect time interval for the slave girl to perfect herself in the art of wearing pantaloons, and all other male rig—the costume she was to wear as a passenger aboard the ship.

Days passed. Weeks. Then a month and a half. During this interval all correspondence referring to the fugitive slave was filled with such terms as: "Is she still running with bleeding feet?" placed there to blind anyone who might attempt to investigate the matter.

At the appointed time, Dr. H. met with Mr. B. (now William Penn) in Washington driving a horse and carriage and prepared for doing his duty.

Then Still received this letter from William Penn:

135

My Dear Sir:—A recent letter from my friend, probably has led you to expect this from me. He was delighted to receive yours of the 23d, stating that the boy was *all right*. He found the "Prof. gentleman" a *perfect gentleman;* cool, quiet, thoughtful, and *perfectly competent to execute his undertaking.* At the first three minutes of their interview, he felt assured that all would be right. He, and all concerned, give you and that gentlemen sincere thanks for what you have done. May the blessings of Him, who cares for the poor, be on your heads. . . .

Wm. Penn

Perseverance had paid dividends for William Penn. The presence of the doctor brought a sense of relief. With everything arranged, the horse and carriage stood before the White House (William Penn preferred this place as a starting point rather than from his own office door). The slave girl—"Joe"—was to act as coachman while they passed through Washington. When "he" was called, he appeared displaying a natural and polite manner. Then he jumped quickly into the carriage and took the reins and whip in his hands while the doctor and William Penn were exchanging farewells and shaking hands.

The order was given to Joe, "Drive on!" as the doctor took the seat beside the "boy."

As the horse trotted off, the doctor sat in his carriage as composed as if he had just received an honorable and lucrative office from the White House and was returning home to tell his wife the good news.

Once outside of Washington, the doctor took the reins in his hands because he had much more experience of the roads than his coachman. Maryland—the state through which they had to travel—was familiar to him since he had lived there in his earlier days for a time. He knew, also, that his horse would need food and water before they reached Pennsylvania.

It was clear they would have to spend one or two nights, at the very least, in Maryland, either at a tavern or farm-house.

Then he remembered a farmer whose house was on the road they traveled. This slaveholder's place lay about a day's journey away. The doctor could think of nothing better than to renew the old acquaintance he had made when he was a young man.

Night fell, after a day's travel; and the doctor with his "boy" knocked on the farmer's door. The farmer and his family remembered him at once and proceeded to welcome his warmly. As a matter of strategy, he responded by making a "fuss over them." But at the same time, he did not fail to assume airs of importance, calculated to make them think he had grown older and wiser since the time they first met. After a hearty meal, the conversation fell to farming, in all its branches, as well as the care and keeping of "niggers." Finally, he spoke of medicine and its modern advances, which left the family exceedingly flattered and honored to be visited by such a distinguished doctor.

The evening passed pleasantly, with the doctor in the parlor and "Joe" in the kitchen. But "Joe" had been schooled carefully, "precept upon precept, here a little, and there a little," as to how he should act in the presence of his master, white people, or slaves. Therefore, he acted his role with expertise.

The farmer insisted on giving them a night's lodging.

Before the evening grew late, the doctor feared some ac-

137

cident might shatter his excellent luck. To counteract this, he intimated he felt a "little languid," and wanted to retire early. And since he was "liable to vertigo," and was not quite well, needed his "boy Joe" close by at all times. He asked for his servant to sleep in his room.

"Simply give him a bed quilt and he will fare well enough in one corner of the room," said the doctor.

His host agreed readily; and soon the doctor was in bed, sleeping soundly, and Joe, wrapped up in a bed quilt, was in the corner of the room, quite comfortable.

The next morning the doctor arose at an early hour, as was prudent for a gentleman of his position, and feeling refreshed, partook of a good breakfast. Then he, and his boy Joe climbed into the wagon, turning face, eyes, hope, and steps Pennsylvania-ward. At just what time they crossed Mason and Dixon's line was blurred in his memory. But at four o'clock on Thanksgiving Day, the doctor safely landed the "fleeing girl of fifteen" at the home of William Still in Philadelphia.

The doctor said to Mrs. Still, who came to the door, "I wish to leave this young lad with you a short while, and I will call and see further about him." Without any more explanation he stepped into his carriage and drove away, evidently anxious to return to his home where his wife awaited his arrival after so many days away.

At the time of the "delivery" William Still happened to be away from home, busy with antislavery work in another place. He returned shortly after the doctor had left.

His wife said to him at his return, "The doctor has been here [he was the family physician] and left this 'young lad,' and said he would call again and see about him."

The "young lad" was sitting quite composed in the dining room with his cap on.

138

Mr. Still turned to him and asked, "I suppose you are the person that the doctor went to Washington after, are you not?"

"No," said Joe.

"Where are you from, then?" was the next question.

"From York, Sir."

"From York? Why then did the doctor bring you here?" was the next question. "The doctor went expressly to Washington after a young girl who was to be brought away dressed up as a boy, and I took you to be the person."

Without replying, the lad arose and walked out of the house. Mr. Still, mystified, followed him, and when the two were alone, the lad said, "I am the one the doctor went after."

After congratulating her, the black Anti-slavery Secretary asked why she had said she was not from Washington, D.C., but from York.

She explained that the doctor had strictly charged her not to own to any person, except William Still himself, that she was from Washington, but from York. As there were some persons present (his wife, Letitia, a hired girl, and a fugitive woman) when the questions were put to her, she felt that it would be a violation of her pledge to answer in the affirmative.

No one in the room, as it turned out, had doubted that she was other than a lad, so well had she acted her part.

She was a prize so rare and remarkable that Mr. Still wanted the other members of the Vigilance Committee to see her. Other interested people were invited—such as stockholders and antislavery men who donated time, advice, and money to the cause of freedom, but who did not necessarily become involved in conducting slaves away. And after a short stay in Philadelphia, she moved on to New York.

Her permanent record in Underground Railroad files reads:

Thanksgiving Day, Nov., 1855

Arrived, Ann Maria Weems, *alias* "Joe Wright," *alias* "Ellen Capron," from Washington, through the aid of Dr. H. She is about fifteen years of age, bright mulatto, well grown, smart and good-looking. For the last three years, or about that length of time, she has been owned by Charles M. Price, a negro trader, of Rockville, Maryland. Mr. P. was given to "intemperance," to a very great extent, and gross "profanity." He buys and sells many slaves in the course of the year. "His wife is cross and peevish." She used to take great pleasure in "torturing" one "little slave boy." He was the son of his master (and was owned by him); this was the chief cause of the mistress' spite.

Ann Maria had always desired her freedom from childhood, and although not thirteen, when first advised to escape, she received the suggestion without hesitation, and ever after that time waited almost daily, for more than two years, the chance to flee. Her friends were, of course, to aid her, and make arrangements for her escape. Her owner, fearing that she might escape, for a long time compelled her to sleep in the chamber with "her master and mistress;" indeed she was so kept until about three weeks before she fled. She left her parents living in Washington. Three of her brothers had been sold South from their parents. Her mother had been purchased for $1,000, and one of her sisters for $1,600 for freedom. Before Ann Maria was thirteen years of age $700 was offered for her by a friend, who desired to procure her freedom, but the offer was promptly refused, as were succeeding ones repeatedly made. The only chance of procuring her freedom, depended upon getting her away on the Underground Rail Road. She was neatly dressed in male habiliments, and in that manner came all the way from Washington. After passing two or three days with her new

140

friends in Philadelphia, she was sent on (in male attire) to Lewis Tappan, of New York, who had likewise been deeply interested in her case from the beginning, and who held himself ready, as was understood, to cash a draft for $300 to compensate the man who might risk his own liberty in bringing her on from Washington. After her arrival safely in New York, she found a home and kind friends in the family of the Rev. A. N. Freeman, [a black minister who lived in Brooklyn] and received quite an ovation characteristic of the Underground Rail Road.

But her safety, even in New York, was in question. Therefore, the decision was made to forward her to Canada, to be educated at the "Buxton Settlement."

chapter eight

At the end of 1855, word reached the Anti-slavery office that Captain Lambson, an Underground Railroad sea captain from Virginia, had been apprehended by the authorities while secreting a cargo of fugitives aboard his ship. He lay in prison awaiting sentence.

Powerless to help him, the members of the Vigilance Committee began to collect what little money they could to be used for his defense.

In a letter to Thomas Garrett in Wilmington, Delaware, who was deeply interested in the fate of the unfortunate Lambson, William Still related what was being done in Philadelphia.

This reply came from Garrett:

Wilmington, 5 mo. 11th, 1855

Esteemed Friends—McKim and Still.—

. . . Captain Lambson is desirous of having sent him a book, or books, with the strongest arguments of the noted men of the South against the institution of Slavery, as he wishes to prepare to defend himself, as he has little confidence in his attorney. Cannot you send me something that

142

will be of benefit to him, or send it direct to him. Would not W. Goodell's book be of use? His friends here think there is no chance for him but to go to the penitentiary.

They now refuse to let any one but his attorney see him.

As ever, your friend,
Thos. Garrett

But Captain Lambson was tried, convicted, and sent to the penitentiary.

Most seafaring ventures in the Underground Railroad, however, while dangerous, were successful.

About the 4th of July, 1856, a message reached William Still that a schooner containing fifteen Underground Railroad passengers from Norfolk, Virginia, would be landed near League Island, directly at the foot of Broad Street, that evening at a late hour. A request accompanied the message, to the effect that the Committee be on hand to receive them. The Secretary procured three carriages, with trustworthy drivers, and between ten and eleven o'clock at night arrived on the banks of the Schuylkill, where all was quiet as a "country grave-yard." The moon was shining, and so the mast of a schooner was seen. No other vessel was in sight. The hearts of those on board swelled with joy; but as they were still in danger, no one dared utter a word above a whisper. The captain disclosed his name and that of the vessel to the Committee members, who thought to jump down on its deck. But as the embankment slanted too sharply for safety, they decided instead to pull the fugitives from the deck up the embankment.

One after the other were pulled up and greeted warmly. Then came the turn of one large woman, weighing about two hundred and sixty pounds—large enough to make two average women. The captain, who had experienced much

143

inconvenience with her on the voyage, owing to the space she required, chuckled over the fact that the Committee would have their hands full for once. Poor Mrs. Walker stretched out her large arms, which William Still and the others grasped. The captain laughed heartily as did the other passengers at the tug now being made. They pulled with a will. Mrs. Walker remained on the deck. The pullers took breath, and again took hold, this time calling upon the captain to give a helping hand. The captain did so, placing himself in position for pushing to the full extent of his powers, and finally she was safely landed. The runaways entered the carriages and were taken to several homes where they were comfortably provided for.

The voyage, though successful, had presented more than the ordinary number of dangers. Even before sailing from Norfolk, the fugitives were nearly caught while waiting for a small boat to take them to the schooner. Just on the edge of the river, where they waited under cover of darkness, they imagined they heard watchmen approaching. In order to evade these men, they all slipped into the river, the water being shallow, and within the shadow of another craft. There they remained for an hour and a half. They were thoroughly soaked, though nothing more. About ten o'clock a small oyster boat came to their relief, and all were soon placed aboard the schooner, which was loaded with corn and other cargo. All, with the exception of the large woman, and one other woman, were required to enter a hole apparently leading through the bottom of the boat, but in reality a compartment expressly constructed for the Underground Railroad business.

The entrance was not large enough for Mrs. Walker, so she, along with another woman who was thought "too fat" to endure the close confinement, was secreted behind some corn in back of the cabin, a place so secluded that only well-experienced searchers would be likely to find it. In this way the captain put to sea. After some fifteen hours he thought it safe to bring his passengers up on deck where they could inhale pure air—which was greatly needed, as they were near to suffocation. The change of air had such an effect on one of the passengers that, in his excitement, he refused to conform to orders. But the captain threatened to throw him overboard and the man lowered his voice. Before reaching a lock the captain, supposing that they might be in danger from contact with boats and men, again called them "to go into their hole" under the deck. Not even the big woman was excused now. She pleaded that she could not get through, but her companions insisted that she try, for the safety of all concerned. One of the more resolute sisters said, "She must take off her clothes then; it will never do having her stay upon the deck to betray all the rest." And this stand being unanimous, the poor woman had to comply; and except for a single undergarment, she was as bare as Eve in the Garden of Eden. With the help of passengers below, she was squeezed through, but not without considerable bruising where the rub was severest. All were now below the deck, the well-fitting oilcloth was put over the hole, and a heavy table set over it. When they came within sight of the lock no humans were visible above the schooner but the captain, the mate, and a small boy—the son of the captain. At the lock, not unexpectedly, three officers came aboard the boat and ordered it stopped. The captain was told that they had received a telegraphic dispatch from Norfolk that his boat was suspected of having slaves secreted on it. They talked with the captain and the mate for a considerable while, and closely examined the boy, but gained no information except that "the yellow fever had been raging very bad in Norfolk." The officers seemed alarmed at this fever news, and they lost no time in attending to their official errand. They searched the cabin where the two fat women were first secreted. Then the other parts of the boat were searched. Then they began to take up the hatchways, but the place was so permeated with foul air that the men started back and declared that nobody could live in such a place, and swore that it smelled like the yellow fever. At that, the captain invited them to search to their heart's content. The officers concluded that there were no slaves aboard because nobody could live there, asked for their charges (three dollars) which the laws of the State of Virginia required for performing said duty, thanked the captain, and left the vessel.

Throughout the entire episode not a sound came from any of the fugitives. The children had been put under the influence of alcohol to prevent their crying out. The others endured their hour of agony with patience until the lock was safely passed, and the river reached. Fresh air was then allowed them and the great danger was considered over. But the captain wisely decided to land his cargo at League Island instead of at the wharves of Philadelphia. The passengers testified that Captain B. was very kind. They were noted in Still's records as:

ISAAC, was about fifty years of age, dark, tall, well-made, intelligent, and was owned by George Brown, who resided at Deep Creek. Isaac testified that said Brown invariably treated him cruelly. For thirty years Isaac had hired his time, found himself food, clothing, and everything, yet as he had advanced in years, neither his task, nor his hire was diminished, but on the contrary his hire of late years had been increased. He winced under the pressure, and gave himself up to the study of the Underground Rail Road. While

146

arrangements for fleeing were pending, he broke the secret to his wife, Polly, in whom he trusted; she being true to freedom, although sorrowing to part with him, threw no obstacle in his way. Besides his wife, he had also two daughters, Amanda A. and Mary Jane, both slaves. Nevertheless, having made up his mind not to die a slave, he resolved to escape at all hazards.

HENDERSON belonged to the estate of A. Briggs, which was about to be settled, and knowing he was accounted on the inventory as personal property, he saw that he too would be sold with the rest of the movables, if he was not found among the missing.

He began to consider what he had endured as a slave, and came to the conclusion that he had had "a rugged road to hoe all the way along" and that he might have it much worse if he waited to be sold. In obeying this call he suffered the loss of his wife, Julia, and two children, who were fortunately free. Henderson was about thirty-one years of age, stout, and of healthy appearance, worth in cash perhaps $1200.

WILLIAM was thirty-four years of age, of a chestnut color, substantial physical structure, and of good faculties. The man who professed to own him he called William Taylor, and "he was a very hard man, one of the kind which could not be pleased, nor give a slave a pleasant answer one time in fifty." Being thoroughly sick of William Taylor, he fell in love with the Underground Rail Road and Canada.

MRS. WALKER, the big fat woman, was thirty-eight years of age, and a pleasant-looking person, of a very dark hue. Besides the struggles already alluded to, she was obliged to leave her husband. Of her master she declared that she could "say nothing good." His name was Arthur Cooper, of Georgetown; but she had never lived with him, however; for twenty years she had hired her time, paying five dollars per month. When young she scarcely thought of the gross wrongs that were heaped upon her; but as she grew older, and thought more about her condition, she scouted the idea that God had designed her to be a slave, and decided that she would be one to leave Dixey in the first Underground Rail Road train that might afford her the chance. She determined not to remain even for the sake of her husband, who was a slave. With such a will, therefore, she started. Upon leaving Philadelphia, she went with the most of her company to Boston, and thence to New Bedford, where she was living when last heard from.

REBECCA LEWEY was the wife of a man who was familiarly known by the name of "Blue Beard," his proper name being Henry Lewey. For a long time, although a slave himself, he was one of the most dexterous managers in the Underground Rail Road agency in Norfolk. . . .

The appearing of Mrs. Lewey was a matter of unusual interest. Although she had worn the yoke, she was gentle in her manners, and healthy-looking, so much so that no life insurance agent would have had need to subject her to medical examination before insuring her. She was twenty-eight years of age, but had never known personal abuse as a slave; she was nonetheless anxious, however, to secure her freedom. Her husband, Blue Beard, judging from certain signs, that he was suspected by slave-holders, and might at any time be caged, (indeed, he had recently been in the lions' den, but got out); in order to save his wife, sent her on in advance as he had decided to follow her soon in a similar manner. Rebecca was not without hope of again meeting her husband. This desire was gratified before many months had passed, as he was fortunate enough to make his way to Canada.

MARY KNIGHT was a single woman, twenty-six years of age, dark, stout, and of pleasing manners; she complained of having been used hard.

148

SARAH SAUNDERS had been claimed as the property of Richard Gatewood, a clerk in the naval services. According to Sarah he was a very clever slave-holder, and had never abused her. Nor was she aware that he had ever treated any of his servants cruelly. Sarah, however, had not lived in Gatewood's immediate family, but had been allowed to remain with her grandmother, rather as a privileged character. She was young, fair, and prepossessing. Having a sister living in Philadelphia, who was known to the agent in Norfolk, Sarah was asked one day if she would not like to see her sister. She at once answered, "Yes." After further conversation the agent told her that if she would keep the matter entirely private, he would arrange for her to go by the Underground Rail Road. Being willing and anxious to go, she promised due obedience to the rules; she was not told, however, how much she would have to pass through on the way, else, according to her own admission, she never would have come as she did; her heart would have failed her. But when the goal was gained, like all others, she soon forgot her sufferings, and rejoiced heartily at getting out of Slavery, even though her condition had not been so bad as that of many others.

SOPHIA GRAY, with her son and daughter, Henry and Mary, was from Portsmouth. The mother was a tall, yellow woman, with well-cut features, about thirty-three years of age, with manners indicative of more than average intelligence. The son and daughter were between twelve and fourteen years of age; well-developed for their age, modest, and finely-formed mulattoes. . . .

They were sent with others to New Bedford, Massachusetts. It was not long after being in New Bedford, before the boy was put to a trade, and the daughter was sent to Boston, where she had an aunt (a fugitive), living in the family of the Hon. George S. Hilliard [the Commissioner who had be-

149

friended Ellen Craft some years before]. Mr. and Mrs. Hilliard were so impressed by Mary's intelligent countenance and her appearance generally, that they decided that she must have a chance for an education, and opened their hearts and home to her. [They enrolled her in the Grammar School, which at the time was composed chiefly of white students.]

Late one evening, William Still received notice that a wooden crate was expected which promised to contain a fugitive slave. He and James McKim planned to receive it.

The advance communication stated that Henry "Box" Brown decided to leave Richmond, Virginia, deciding that his prospects there appeared dim at best. To evade the vigilance of the Virginia slave-hunters, Brown agreed to a most ingenious plan conceived by an Underground Railroad agent in the town. The ordinary modes of travel being too hazardous, he permitted himself to be boxed up and forwarded to Philadelphia by direct express. The measurements of the box were two feet, eight inches deep, two feet wide, and three feet long, and it was lined with baize. For food and water, one bladder of water and a few biscuits were provided. The mechanical instrument to meet the death struggle for fresh air was one large gimlet. The box was nailed up and hooped with five hickory loops and addressed to Wm. H. Johnson, Arch Street, Philadelphia.

"This side up with care" was marked on it and it was sent via Adams Express first in a fray and then overland to Philadelphia, express.

Samuel A. Smith, the man who aided and abetted him, was a shoe dealer in town, and a white man.

It was twenty-six hours from the time he left Richmond until his arrival in Philadelphia. The words "This side up" were not entirely adhered to by the different expressmen, who handled the box in their usual rough manner. At one point, they had the box upside down, forcing the occupant to ride on his head for miles. A day or so before he was expected, a message arrived at a Vigilance Committee's office that a box containing a man might be expected by the three o'clock morning train from the South.

William Still, having become used to meeting and accompanying arrivals, went to the depot at half past two in the morning. Fearing that the slave would be dead, Still looked anxiously while freight was being unloaded from the cars, to see if he could recognize a box containing a man. Then he came upon one about the size to contain a man; but it had the scent of death about it. Upon inquiry, he learned it was not the one he sought, and he heaved a sigh of relief.

That afternoon, he received a telegram from Richmond: "Your case of goods is shipped and will arrive tomorrow morning."

Instead of a member of the Vigilance Committee going to the depot a second time, which might excite suspicion, James McKim felt it best to have the express bring the box directly to the Anti-slavery office.

There was a dilemma facing McKim: that was to get the Adam's Express Company to deliver a box from Richmond addressed to Arch Street, and yet not intended for that street, to the Anti-slavery office at 107 North Fifth St. For an abolitionist to go to the express company and request the new delivery address was out of the question. Applying his usual good judgment, he went to his friend, E. M. Davis, then engaged in the mercantile business and asked his advice. Davis was a member of the Executive Committee of the Pennsylvania Anti-slavery Society, and son-in-law of

James and Lucretia Mott; he had long worked with Adam's Express Office and was familiar with their trade practices and drivers assigned for deliveries, from any part of the country.

"Dan, an Irishman, one of Adam's Express drivers, is just the fellow to go to the depot after the box," said Davis. "He drinks a little too much whiskey sometimes, but he will do anything I ask him to do, promptly and obligingly. I'll trust Dan, for I believe he is the very man."

It was agreed that Dan should go after the box next morning, before daylight and bring it to the Anti-slavery office direct. And to make it all the more agreeable for Dan to get up out of his warm bed and go on this errand before daybreak, they decided to give him a five-dollar gold piece for himself.

Next morning, according to plan, the box was at the Anti-slavery office. Present to behold the resurrection were J. M. McKim, Professor C. D. Cleveland, Lewis Thompson, and William Still.

Mr. McKim, deeply interested for a long time in any antislavery triumph, stood over the box perfectly composed.

Professor Cleveland, although his interest in the slave had, till now, been remote in terms of actual encounter with the fugitives, found his emotions overpowering.

Mr. Thompson, of the firm of Merrihew & Thompson, printers of such incendiary documents in Philadelphia as antislavery papers and pamphlets, was composed and ready to witness the scene.

All was quiet. The door had been safely locked. Now the proceedings began. Mr. McKim rapped softly on the lid, and called out, "All right!" Instantly came the answer from within, "All right, Sir!"

152

They were astounded. With saw and hatchet they cut the five hickory loops. Off came the lid. Then the marvelous resurrection of Brown ensued. He rose up in his box and reached out his hand, saying, "How do you do, gentlemen?"

Dripping with perspiration, he was about as wet as if he had come up from the Delaware. To the men who stood with mouth agape, he sang: "I waited patiently for the Lord, and He heard my prayer." He sang the psalm in such a manner as to charm his astonished audience.

Immediately, he was christened Henry Box Brown. And following the ceremony he went to the homes of James Mott and E. M. Davis on Ninth St. where he was cordially received.

But, as he had been for so long doubled up in a box, he felt the urge to walk about in the fresh air. With James Mott wearing a broad-brimmed hat and strolling by his side, he promenaded the yard in the greatest of spirits.

Then he went to William Still's home, leaving the Motts' after a stay of two days. Shortly thereafter he departed for Boston, leaving behind those who witnessed this strange resurrection with feelings of elation as well as sympathy for the fugitive who would go to such lengths to be free.

The man who boxed him up rejoiced also. But his victory led him to render similar service to two other bondsmen, and, unfortunately, the undertaking in this instance proved to be a complete failure. Samuel A. Smith was arrested, imprisoned, and suffered severely, as may be seen from the following news item in the New York *Tribune,* written upon his release from the penitentiary.

THE DELIVERER OF BOX BROWN—MEETING OF THE COLORED CITIZENS OF PHILADELPHIA

Samuel A. Smith, who boxed up Henry Box Brown in Richmond, Va., and forwarded him by overland express to Philadelphia, and who was arrested and convicted . . . for boxing up two other slaves, also directed to Philadelphia, having served out his imprisonment in the Penitentiary, was released on the 18th ultimo, and arrived in this city on the 21st.

Though he lost all his property; though he was refused witnesses on his trial (no officer could be found, who would serve a summons on a witness); though for five long months, in hot weather, he was kept heavily chained in a cell four by eight feet in dimensions; though he received five dreadful stabs, aimed at his heart, by a bribed assassin, nevertheless he still rejoices in the motives which prompted him to "undo the heavy burdens, and let the oppressed go free." Having resided nearly all his life in the South, where he had traveled and seen much of the "peculiar institution," and had witnessed the most horrid enormities inflicted upon the slave, whose cries were ever ringing in his ears, and for whom he had the warmest sympathy, Mr. Smith could not refrain from believing that the black man, as well as the white, had God-given rights. Consequently, he was not accustomed to shed tears when a poor creature escaped from his "kind master;" nor was he willing to turn a deaf ear to his appeals and groans, when he knew he was thirsting for freedom. From 1828 up to the day he was incarcerated, many had sought his aid and counsel, nor had they sought in vain. In various places he operated with success. In Richmond, however, it seemed expedient to invent a new plan for certain emergencies, hence the Box and Express plan was devised, at the instance of a few heroic slaves, who had manifested their willingness to die in a box, on the road to liberty, rather than continue longer under the yoke. But these heroes fell into the power of their enemies. Mr. Smith had not long been

154

in the Penitentiary before he had fully gained the esteem and confidence of the Superintendent and other officers. Finding him to be humane and generous-hearted—showing kindness toward all, especially in buying bread, &c., for the starving prisoners, and by a timely note of warning, which had saved the life of one of the keepers, for whose destruction a bold plot had been arranged—the officers felt disposed to show him such favors as the law would allow. But their good intentions were soon frustrated. The Inquisition (commonly called the Legislature), being in session in Richmond, hearing that the Superintendent had been speaking well of Smith, and circulating a petition for his pardon, indignantly demanded to know if the rumor was well founded. Two weeks were spent by the Inquisition, and many witnesses were placed upon oath, to solemnly testify in the matter. One of the keepers swore that his life had been saved by Smith. Col. Morgan, the Superintendent, frequently testified in writing and verbally to Smith's good deportment; acknowledging that he had circulated petitions, &c.; and took the position, that he sincerely believed, that it would be to the interest of the institution to pardon him, calling the attention of the Inquisition, at the same time, to the fact, that not unfrequently pardons had been granted to criminals, under sentence of death, for the most cold-blooded murder, to say nothing of other gross crimes. The effort for pardon was soon abandoned, for the following reason given by the Governor: "I can't, and I won't pardon him."

In view of the unparalleled injustice which Mr. S. had suffered, as well as on the account of the aid he had rendered to the slaves, on his arrival in this city the colored citizens of Philadelphia felt that he was entitled to sympathy and aid, and straightway invited him to remain a few days, until arrangements could be made for a mass meeting to receive him. Accordingly, on last Monday evening, a mass meeting convened in the Israel church, and the Rev. Wm. T. Catto

155

was called to the chair, and Wm. Still was appointed secretary. The chairman briefly stated the object of the meeting. Having lived in the South, he claimed to know something of the workings of the oppressive system of slavery generally, and declared that, notwithstanding the many exposures of the evil which came under his own observation, the most vivid descriptions fell far short of the realities his own eyes had witnessed. He then introduced Mr. Smith, who arose and in a plain manner briefly told his story, assuring the audience that he had always hated slavery, and has taken great pleasure in helping many out of it, and though he had suffered much physically and pecuniarily for the cause's sake, yet he murmured not, but rejoiced in what he had done. After taking his seat, addresses were made by the Rev. S. Smith, Messrs. Kinnard, Brunner, Bradway, and others. The following preamble and resolutions were adopted—

WHEREAS, We, the colored citizens of Philadelphia, having among us Samuel A. Smith, who was incarcerated over seven years in the Richmond Penitentiary, for doing an act that was honorable to his feelings and his sense of justice and humanity, therefore,

Resolved, That we welcome him to this city as a martyr to the cause of Freedom.

Resolved, That we heartily tender him our gratitude for the good he has done to the suffering race.

Resolved, That we sympathize with him in his losses and sufferings in the cause of the poor, down-trodden slave.

W. S.

While in Philadelphia, he stayed with the Still family.

Some money was collected for him, for which he was very grateful. Then Mr. Smith was married to a lovely lady who had waited patiently for him while he lay in prison. The minister, William Furness, wished the happy

156

couple the best from life as they departed for western New York where they planned to make their home.

The persecuted Underground Railroad man reaffirmed, as he left his friends in Philadelphia, that he had retained an unshaken belief that in aiding his fellow man to be free, he was obeying the highest of laws.

chapter nine

William Still had witnessed suffering fugitives, but never had he seen one die. Early in 1857 a man named Romulus Hall reached his office with a case of frostbite so severe he had lost all feeling in his feet. Mrs. Still found a bed for him in an attic room. There the dying man rested while Underground Railroad doctors administered what aid they could.

For the first week he seemed to improve.

During this period, William Still visited him frequently. He tried not only to cheer his flagging spirits, but he also wanted to ask Hall about the ordeal that resulted in his grave physical state.

The emaciated black man nestled in the soft pillows and told the whole tragic tale.

In March, 1857, Abrams Harris fled from John Henry Suthern, who lived near Benedict, Charles County, Maryland, where he engaged in farming and was the owner of about seventy slaves. He kept an overseer who administered almost daily floggings on males and females, old and young. Abrams, dejected by this treatment, decided to seek out the Underground Railroad. If it had not been for the strong attachment he had for his wife, who was owned by a man named Samuel Adams, and who was "pretty well treated," he never would have "suffered as he did."

But soon, even this held no comfort for him. Therefore, Abrams consulted with his fellow servant, Romulus Hall. Hall had an alias—George Weems. These two friends decided to chance running off. Each had a wife he had to "tear himself away from," and each was equally ignorant of the distance they had to travel and the dangers and suffering to be endured. But they decided to "trust in the Lord" and kept the North Star in view. For nine days and nights, without a guide, they traveled at a very exhausting rate, enduring cold weather and fasting several days at a time. Romulus Hall, about fifty, weakened by hunger and cold, had to be left along the way.

Abrams arrived at the Committee in Philadelphia. He told of his life on the farm with his master:

Master and Mistress very frequently visited the Presbyterian Church but were not members. Mistress was very bad. About three weeks before I left, the overseer, in a violent fit of bad temper, shot and badly wounded a young slave by the name of Henry Waters, but no sooner than he got well enough he escaped, and had not been heard of up to the time I left. About three years before this happened, an overseer of my master was found shot to death on the road. At once, some of the slaves were suspected, and were all taken to the Court House, at Serentown, St. Mary's county; but all came off clear. After this occurrence a new overseer, by the name of John Deckett, was employed. Although his predecessor had been dead three years, Deckett, nevertheless, concluded that it was not "too late" to flog the secret out of some of the slaves. Accordingly, he selected a young man for his vic-

159

tim, and flogged him so cruelly that he could scarcely walk
or stand, and to keep from being actually killed, the boy
told an untruth, and confessed that he and his uncle Henry
killed Webster, the overseer; whereupon the poor fellow was
sent to jail to be tried for his life.

But Abrams did not wait for the verdict. He reached
the Committee where Still noted him for the records as a
man of medium size, tall, dark chestnut color, who could
read and write a little and was quite intelligent. He was
furnished a free ticket to Canada and other assistance.

In fact, it was just a few days after Abrams had gone on
to Canada that Romulus Hall was brought to the Vigilance
Committee by a pitying stranger, arriving in a most shocking condition.

William Still marveled that he had been able to reach
the city at all. On his arrival he provided medical and other
necessary comforts for him. The doctors and all concerned
hoped he would be able to regain his health, allowing for
the possibility of loss of his toes. For one whole week he
seemed to be improving. But at the end of that time, his
symptoms changed, indicating not only the end of slavery
for him but the end of all his earthly troubles.

Lockjaw developed in a most malignant form, and for
nearly thirty-six hours the unfortunate victim suffered in
extreme agony, though not a murmur escaped him for having brought it upon himself in seeking his liberty. He endured the sight of death in a remarkably resigned manner.

Loathe to do so, but thinking it valuable, William Still
sat next to his bed in the darkened room and asked for
testimony relative to his escape.

"Do you regret having attempted to leave slavery?"
asked the empathetic Chairman.

160

Still got up and walked toward the door when the man didn't reply.

The stricken black man remained silent a long while before he gasped after a severe spasm, "Don't go; I have not answered your question. I am glad I escaped from slavery!"

Still returned to his bedside.

The dying man attempted to give his name and that of his master, but was too weak to be understood.

Heartsick that slavery could exist and leave behind victims such as this, the black Chairman of the Acting Committee regarded the man who lay there dying in a strange land among strangers.

Following his death, the Anti-slavery members decided to keep the burial private except for a few friends of the Committee. Nevertheless, they arranged a decent burial in the beautiful Lebanon Cemetery.

When the friends of the fugitive, Drs. J. L. Griscom and H. T. Childs, whose faithful services were freely given, and Mrs. H. S. Duterte and Mrs. Williams, who generously performed the offices of charity and friendship at his burial, met at Still's office, they found in Hall's purse one single five-cent piece—his whole pecuniary worth.

His name was marked on the records as the first death on the Underground Railroad in the Philadelphia region.

Soon afterward, a letter was received from his companion, who had been more fortunate, having reached Canada. In part he said:

"I am enjoying good health, and hope when this reaches you, you may be enjoying the same blessing. Give my love to Mr. ——, and tell him I am in a land of liberty! I am a man among men!"

The letter was addressed to the deceased.

It fell to Still to inform Abrams of his friend's death.

Shortly after, a reply written by Reverend L. D. Mansfield on behalf of Abrams tells of his sad feeling on hearing of his friend's death. In this minister, the antislavery cause had one of those rare men who believed it right "to do unto others as one would be done by" in practice, not in theory only, and who felt that they could not be excused for "falling down," in obedience to the Fugitive Slave Law, any more than Daniel could for worshiping the "golden image" under Nebuchadnezzar.

Auburn, New York, May 4th, 1857

Dear Br. Still:—Henry Lemmon wishes me to write to you in regard to your kind letter, conveying the intelligence of the death of your fugitive guest, Geo. Weems. He was deeply affected at the intelligence, for he was most devotedly attached to him and had been for many years. Mr. Lemmon now expects his sister to come on, and wishes you to aid her in any way in your power—as he knows you will.

He wishes you to send the coat and cap of Weems by his sister when she comes. And when you write out the history of Weems' escape, and it is published, that you would send him a copy of the papers. He has not been very successful in getting work yet. . . .

Mr. Lemmon sends his respects to you and Mrs. Still. Give my kind regards to her and accept also yourself.

Yours very truly,
L. D. Mansfield

When, indeed, the publication of Romulus Hall's death reached beyond Philadelphia, it brought responses from the abolitionists such as this from Thomas Garrett in Wilmington: "I was truly sorry to hear of the fate of that poor fellow who had perilled so much for liberty. I was in hopes

162

from what thee told me, that he would recover with the loss, perhaps, of some of his toes."

Henry Predo fled from Buckstown, Dorchester County, Maryland, in March, 1857. Physically, Henry was a giant. About twenty-seven years of age, he was stout and well-made, quite black and no fool. His master had threatened to sell him a short time before he had escaped. To avoid this fate, he decided to try his luck on the Underground Railroad—in company with seven others. The six men and two women started for Canada. For two or three days and nights they managed to outwit all their adversaries.

In the meantime, however, a reward of three thousand dollars was offered for their arrest. The temptation was too great to be resisted by the man who had been entrusted with the care of them, and who had promised to pilot them to a place of safety.

One night, through the treachery of their Underground Railroad agent, they were all taken into Dover jail, where the sheriff and several deputies who had been notified beforehand by the traitor waited to receive them. They were led upstairs in the building while the betrayer remarked all the while that they were "cold, but would soon have a good warming." Once the light was lit they discovered the bars on the windows—and the fact that they had been betrayed. Though resisted brutally by the sheriff with a revolver in his hand, they fought their way down the steps, and in the stir of excitement, as good luck would have it, they plunged into the sheriff's private apartment where his wife and children were sleeping. The wife cried lustily! A shovel full of fire, to the great danger of burning the building, was scattered over the room. Out of the window jumped the two female fugitives! Henry, seizing a heavy andiron, smashed out an entire window through which the others

163

leaped a distance of twelve feet. Next they surmounted the wall about the premises.

At this stage of the proceedings, Henry found himself outside the wall; but, at the same time, he lost sight of his comrades. The last enemy he remembered seeing was the sheriff running in his stockings without his shoes. The lawman aimed his pistol at the fugitives. But it did not go off. Six of the others got off, marvelously; where the eighth went was not known.

Daniel Hughes was one of the eight. His owner was Richard Meredith, a farmer. In features he was strong, intelligent, and possessing a thirst for freedom. He stated his reasons for fleeing: "Worked hard in all sorts of weather —in rain and snow." Therefore, he decided to go "where the colored man was free." His master was considered the hardest man around. His mistress was "eighty-three years of age, drank hard," and was "very stormy," and "a member of the Methodist Church." He left brothers and sisters, and uncles and aunts behind. In the combat at the prison he played a manly part.

Thomas Elliott was also one of the brave eight who broke out of Dover jail. He was about twenty-three years of age, alert, and of a superb black complexion. He too had been owned by Richard Meredith. He swore vengeance against the betrayer, a black man, if the opportunity ever presented itself. He left only one living brother. His father and mother were dead.

The faithful abolitionist Thomas Garrett was anxious over the betrayal, as shown in this letter which came to the attention of Still in Philadelphia although it was written to their colleague, the Quaker, Samuel Rhoads, "a stockholder" on the Underground Railroad in the same city.

While not a conductor who came in close contact with fugitive slaves, he had dedicated his energies to promoting the use of Free Produce, or non-slave-grown products, hoping thereby to undermine slavery in the United States. His friendship with individuals in England, such as A. H. Richardson, the antislavery minded Britisher, had resulted in a small, but helpful source of money to aid the destitute black.

Wilmington, 3d mo. 13th, 1857

Dear Cousin, Samuel Rhoads:—I have a letter this day from an agent of the Underground Rail Road, near Dover, in this state, saying I must be on the look out for six brothers and two sisters, they were decoyed and betrayed, he says by a colored man named Thomas Otwell, who pretended to be their friend, and sent a *white scamp* ahead to wait for them at Dover till they arrived; they were arrested and put in Jail there, with Tom's assistance, and some officers. On third day morning about four o'clock, they broke jail; six of them are secreted in the neighborhood, and the writer has not known what became of the other two. The six were to start last night for this place. I hear that their owners have persons stationed at several places on the road watching. I fear they will be taken. If they could lay quiet for ten days or two weeks, they might then get up safe. I shall have two men sent this evening some four or five miles below to keep them away from this town, and send them (if found to Chester County). Thee may show this to Still and McKim, and oblige thy cousin,

Thomas Garrett

Not much more concerning this incident reached the Anti-slavery office until a colored conductor wrote the following letter to William Still:

165

Camden, Del., March 23d, 1857

Dear Sir:—I tak my pen in hand to write to you, to inform you what we have had to go throw for the last two weaks. Thir wir six men and two women was betraid on the tenth of this month, thea had them in prison but thea got out was conveyed by a black man, he told them he wood bring them to my hows, as he wos told, he had ben ther Befor, he has com with Harrett, a woman that stops at my hous when she pases tow and throw yau. You don't no me I supos, the Rev. Thomas H. Kennard dos, or Peter Lowis. He Road Camden Circuit, this man led them in Dover prisin and left them with a whit man; but tha tour out the winders and jump out, so cum back to camden. We put them throug, we hav to carry them 19 mils and cum bak the sam night wich maks 38 mils. It is tou much for our littel horses. We must do the bes we can, ther is much Bisness dun on this Road. We hav to go throw dover and smerny, the two wors places this sid of mary land lin. If you have herd or sean them ples let me no. I will Com to Phila be for long and then I will call and se you. There is much to do her. Ples to wright, I Remain your frend,

Remember me to Thom. Kennard.

William Brinkly

The balance of these brave fugitives, although not named in this connection, succeeded in getting off safely. But how the betrayer, sheriff, and hunters fared was never made known to the Committee.

The escape from Dover jail occupied the busy Vigilance Committee until one of Harriet Tubman's fugitives came to its attention.

A passenger by the name of Samuel Green (alias Wesley Kinnard) left Indian Creek, Chester County, Maryland, where he was held to service or labor by Dr. James Muse.

166

One week elapsed from the time he set out till the time he reached Philadelphia on August 28, 1854. Since he was very intelligent he had managed to read and write a little, contrary to both law and custom. Sam was about twenty-five years of age, and a blacksmith by trade. Although his general character for sobriety, industry, and religion had been considered good, by running away he fell below the limit of forgiveness by the slaveholders of Indian Creek.

At the Vigilance Committee, he stated in a calm and businesslike way that his master, "Dr. James Muse is thought by the servants to be the worst man in Maryland, inflicting whipping and all manner of cruelties upon the servants." Indeed, for several years Sam had been hired out by the doctor at blacksmithing where he chanced to meet Harriet Tubman. She lit for him the light of freedom and told him of the Underground Railroad. It was new to him, but he decided to heed her advice because he saw her as a sister of humanity. Harriet, a shrewd and fearless agent, knew the entire route from that part of the country leading to Canada. In the previous spring, she had paid a visit to the very neighborhood in which Sam lived, expressly to lead her own brothers out of "Egypt." He waited till the way was opened for him to travel the same road, and to his joy he succeeded in reaching Philadelphia.

The Committee, perceiving that he was smart, active, and promising, did not hesitate to write letters of introduction, give him friendly advice, and aid him in the usual manner. He was forwarded on his way. He left a father, mother, and one sister behind. Samuel and Catherine were the names of his parents. And at the time, it seemed that his escape would not affect his parents, nor was it apparent in any way that the owner might seek to revenge himself.

167

The father was an old local preacher in the Methodist Church. He was much esteemed and regarded as inoffensive. He walked the narrow road allotted colored people, bond or free, without exciting a spirit of ill-will in the proslavery power of his community. But the rancor awakened in the breast of slaveholders in consequence of the step taken by his son brought hate and suspicion upon the head of the father. They watched for an occasion to pounce upon him. It was not long before they found their chance.

The old man decided to visit his son, for he was a free Negro, to see how he was faring in a distant land among strangers. He went to Canada and found his son doing well —industrious, a man of sober character, and following in his father's footsteps religiously. He was overjoyed. But he had no way of knowing what his visit would cost him. During the best portion of his days he had worn the yoke of slavery, and had finally purchased his freedom. He innocently believed he had done no wrong. But the enemy lurked in ambush for him, and not long after his return home, he was visited at night by some "gentlemen."

The following excerpt, taken from the Cambridge (Md.) *Democrat* of April 29th, 1857, shows the extent to which proslavery powers were prepared to go:

> The case of the State against Sam Green (free negro) indicted for having in his possession, papers, pamphlets and pictorial representations, having a tendency to create discontent, etc., among the people of color in the State, was tried before the court on Friday last.
>
> This case was of the utmost importance, and has created in the public mind a great deal of interest—it being the first case of the kind ever having occurred in our country.
>
> It appeared, in evidence, that this Green has a son in Canada, to whom Green made a visit last summer. Since his

return to this county, suspicion has fastened upon him, as giving aid and assisting slaves who have since absconded and reached Canada, and several weeks ago, a party of gentlemen from New Market district, went at night, to Green's house and made search, whereupon was found a volume of "Uncle Tom's Cabin," a map of Canada, several schedules of routes to the North, and a letter from his son in Canada, detailing the pleasant trip he had, the number of friends he met on the way, with plenty to eat, drink, etc., and concludes with a request to his father, that he shall tell certain other slaves, naming them, to come on, which slaves, it is well known, did leave shortly afterwards, and have reached Canada. The case was argued with great ability, the counsel on both sides displaying a great deal of ingenuity, learning and eloquence. The first indictment was for the having in possession the letter, map and route schedules. . . .

When it became known to members of the community in which Green lived that he had in his possession these documents, they immediately believed he had a hand in running off slaves. But it was the opinion of the court that the law under which he had been indicted was not applicable to the case and that a verdict of "not guilty" would have to be rendered.

He was arraigned upon another indictment, for having in his possession a copy of *Uncle Tom's Cabin*. In this case, the assistant counsel for the state declared that "Slavery must be protected or it must be abolished," while the legislators sought amendments of the existing statutes to clarify the existing laws.

The May 20th edition of the same newspaper published the outcome of Green's case:

In the case of the State against Sam Green, (free negro) who was tried at the April term of the Circuit Court of this

169

county, for having in his possession abolition pamphlets, among which was "Uncle Tom's Cabin," has been found guilty by the court, and sentenced to the penitentiary for the term of ten years—until the 14th of May, 1867.

The son, hearing the distressing news of his father's fate, wrote to the Vigilance Committee often for help from them for his deliverance. But the Committee was unable to help him. The gates of the penitentiary slammed behind the older man.

Antislavery men in Philadelphia were deeply indebted to the Baltimore *Sun* for the help it unwittingly gave to them. The money spent for the subscription was considered money well spent. This paper used to advertise for runaway slaves from the upper South and border states, showing a small sketch of a black man running with a bundle on his back. A description was given in detail along with the amount of reward offered for his return to the master, whose name and address appeared below the ad.

William Still, who did much of the scanning of the newspaper, kept some of these ads and sent some on to friends and stockholders of the Railroad when they asked for them. Antislavery men as far away as England often requested copies of the slave advertisements in order to see for themselves how the South encouraged the "fine arts."

With more and more slaves running away, slaveholders intended to use every means possible to prevent this loss of property now beginning to run into the hundreds of thousands of dollars. More than fifty slaves passed through the Philadelphia office in a fortnight now.

They came not only from the states nearby, but from cities such as Richmond, Virginia, which furnished a larger number of alert and "likely looking" slaves—as noted by

Still in his record book—than any other one city in the South. It was not surprising, then, that abolitionists were held in great hatred by the slaveholders in that city.

And every so often a slave from the deep South made it onto free soil, from the Southern Market, as it was called in the slave-trading circles. But because the arrival of a fugitive from this region of the South was rare, whenever one managed to make his way to the Anti-slavery office in Philadelphia, William Still regarded the story as an especially valuable piece of information. It furnished the Committee with background material on the institution they hated so much.

One such fugitive, Jim, told about the severe lashings endured by the slaves which opened the flesh wide. He told of life in New Orleans, where female as well as male slaves were laid naked over boxes, while they, grown used to the lash, would remain where they were placed without being tied—awaiting the whip. And he told of the "chain gangs" in constant operation, consisting of four or five slaves chained together at work in the streets, cleaning and sweeping. It was impossible to tell Sunday from Monday there, for the slaves were kept going constantly.

With so many slaves coming through, William Still found little time to dwell on the cruelties inflicted on members of his race. In fact, he and the other members were kept so busy assisting them to Canada, that he made only the briefest notations in the ledger in order to use his time and energies more productively. Often all that remained of the story they told him was their name, the place from which they had escaped, and a few words of description.

The Underground Railroad flourished. Still had noted more than eight hundred arrivals—sixty of them children— from the time he took over the Acting Committee in

December, 1852, until February, 1857. He had in his files almost five hundred letters concerning antislavery affairs. And he had no reason to expect these documents to have any value other than as an aid to future fugitives who might come through, seeking the whereabouts of their loved ones who had gone on ahead.

The year 1857 brought the death of Still's beloved mother. The fugitive slave who had run off twice gave to her dedicated son the inspiration to work for the freedom of his people yet in bonds. That she had suffered in slavery, herself, never left his mind. But that he had been fortunate in having been born free stood in his mind as the opportunity to fight effectively for those less fortunate.

The following year found the Committee and its meager facilities taxed to the utmost in order to accommodate the fugitives. They were occupied with slave affairs day and night.

Still sheltered the slaves and fed them from his table. In fact, it was a rare day when no bondsman sat with his family—if even for a short time—before going on. The Still children—Caroline, Frances, and the two boys—grew used to the presence of fugitives in their home. Their childhood was as intertwined with antislavery work as was the life of their parents. There was no other memory for them save the appearance of strange black people who stayed with them a while and then moved on with others following closely behind.

Often the fugitives arrived at their house in an unclean condition with respect to their physical appearance. Their plantation work clothes smelled of manure. Since they had only one suit of clothes, in most cases, they fled in the coarse garment which they wore as long as it hung together.

But how could it be otherwise, regarding cleanliness, when the very cabins the slaves inhabited were themselves incentives to personal uncleanliness? Granted, in some districts this was more apparent than in others, such as in some parts of Maryland and Delaware, where many fugitives originated. They brought evidence of great neglect on the part of their owners in instilling in them any need for keeping their persons clean.

The one suit which most slaves had was used for working as well as for Sunday. Consequently, if he was sent to ditching one day and got dirty and muddy, and the next day he was ordered to haul manure, he wore his ditching suit. If he was sent into the harvest field the next day, he was obliged to wear his barnyard suit. Frequently such passengers received their first cleaning at the Philadelphia station. Many was the slave who needed a practical lesson before he understood the thoroughness necessary for cleansing himself.

Members of the Committee adopted certain techniques to facilitate this training program. In order to get the message across, they arrived at these persuasions:

"We want to give you some clean clothing, but you need washing before you put them on."

"It will make you feel like a new man to have the dirt of slavery washed off."

"Nothing that could be done for you would make you feel better after the fatigue of travel, than a thorough bath."

"Probably you have not been allowed the opportunity of taking a good bath, and so have not enjoyed one since your mother bathed you."

"Don't be afraid of the water or soap—the harder you rub yourself, the better you will feel."

"Shall we not wash your back and neck for you?"

"I want you to look well while traveling on the Underground Railroad, and not forget from this time forth to try to take care of yourself."

These techniques worked well. With his reticence overcome, the runaway acceded to the proposition—if the water was not too cold. When it was all over the freedman expressed a sense of satisfaction and was truly thankful for this attention.

In this small way, William Still and his associates initiated the more deprived members of his race into the amenities of a new way of life.

In addition to feeding, clothing, and washing the fugitives before they went on to Canada, the members of the Committee attended to another important chore. This was the posting of handbills in various places throughout the city to warn their friends and sympathizers of the presence of slave-catchers who lurked about in ever-increasing numbers.

When such a bounty hunter was discovered to be in Philadelphia or its environs, William Still would get his description and who he worked for, as well as who he sought to take back, and have printed a poster with the information on it, to warn the slave or any person who knew the slave. All this required great haste.

One afternoon, the quiet of the Anti-slavery office was suddenly agitated by the contents of a letter, privately placed in the hands of Mr. McKim by one of the clerks of the Philadelphia *Ledger* office. The letter, it was surmised, was dropped into the box of the *Ledger* office, instead of the U.S. box (one of which was also in the *Ledger* office) by mistake, and seeing that it bore the name of a well-

174

known slave-catcher, Alberti, the clerk had a great desire to know its importance. Whether or not it was sealed, nobody seemed to be sure, but it read that a lady from Maryland was then in Philadelphia, at a boardinghouse on Arch Street, and that she wanted very much to see the above-named Alberti. Her purpose was to catch a fugitive who had arrived in Philadelphia on the Underground Railroad whom she claimed as her property. That she wrote the letter was open for debate; but that it was sent by her consent there was little doubt.

In order to save the fellow from impending doom, no time was to be wasted. A bold move had to be made. But Mr. McKim possessed great ability along those lines. He proposed to find a man who would be willing to answer for Alberti. Such a man was Cyrus Whitson, a member of the Committee, who was able, in James McKim's judgment, to manage the matter successfully. At the time, Whitson was engaged in the Free Labor store, at the corner of Fifth and Cherry streets, near the Anti-slavery office. He came immediately after he was summoned, and Mr. McKim told him the plan, which consisted in visiting the woman in the place of Alberti. He was to find out from her the whereabouts of the fugitive, the names of the witnesses, and all the particulars. Nothing could have delighted the shrewd Whitson any better. Therefore, he started off for the boardinghouse.

Arriving, he rang the bell, and when the servant appeared, he asked if Miss Wilson, from Maryland, was stopping there.

"She is," was the answer.

"I wish to see her."

"Walk in the parlor, Sir."

In went Mr. W., with his big whiskers. Soon Miss Wilson entered the parlor. She was tall, rather fine-looking, and well dressed.

Mr. Whitson, bowing, politely addressed her substantially as follows:

"I have come to see you instead of Mr. George F. Alberti, to whom you addressed a note this morning. Circumstances, over which Mr. Alberti had no control, prevented his coming, so I have come, Madam, to look after your business in his place. Now, Madam, I wish it to be distinctly understood in the outset that whatever transpires between us, so far as this business is concerned, must be kept strictly confidential. By no means, must this matter be allowed to leak out; if it does, the damned abolitionists (excuse me) may ruin me. At any rate, we should not be able to succeed in getting your slave. I am particular on this point, remember."

"You are perfectly right, Sir, indeed I am very glad that your plan is to conduct this matter in this manner, for I do not want my name mixed up with it in any way."

"Very well, Madam, I think we understand each other pretty well. Now please give me the name of the fugitive, his age, size, and color, and where he may be found, how long he has been away, and the witnesses who can be relied on to identify him after he is arrested."

Miss Wilson carefully communicated these important particulars while Mr. Whitson penciled down every word. At the close of the interview he said that the matter would receive his prompt attention and that he saw no difficulty in securing the fugitive.

With that he said, "You shall hear from me soon, Madam, good afternoon." Then he left.

Five minutes after the interview, Whitson was back at

the Anti-slavery office with all Miss Wilson's secrets. First of all, they decided to send a messenger to the place where the fugitive worked to warn him. The man was found and nearly frightened out of his wits. He dropped all and followed the messenger who bore the warning. In the meanwhile, Mr. McKim was preparing, with great dispatch, the following document for the enlightenment and warning of all:

TO WHOM IT MAY CONCERN
BEWARE OF SLAVE-CATCHERS

MISS WILSON, of Georgetown Cross Roads, Kent county, Md., is now in the city in pursuit of her alleged slave man, BUTLER. J. M. Cummings and John Wilson, of the same place, are understood to be here on a similar errand. This is to caution BUTLER and his friends to be on their guard. Let them keep clear of the above-named individuals. Also, let them have an eye on all persons known to be friends of Dr. High, of Georgetown Cross Roads, and Mr. D. B. Cummings, who is not of Georgetown Cross Roads.

It is requested that all parties to whom a copy of this may be sent will post it in a public place, and that the friends of Freedom and Humanity will have the facts herein contained openly read in their respective churches.

"Hide the outcast; betray him not that wandereth." Isaiah xvi 3.

"Thou shalt not deliver unto his master the servant that has escaped from his master unto thee." Deut. xxiii 15.

This was printed as a three-feet-square poster and displayed in large numbers over the city. It attracted much attention and comment. The facts of the document soon found their way to Miss Wilson at her boardinghouse. It was understood, from the description given by a witness, that she was greatly shocked to find her name in everybody's mouth. Without hesitation she started out for "My Maryland," bag in hand.

Thus ended one of the most pleasant interviews that ever took place between a slave-hunter and the Vigilance Committee of Philadelphia.

Engravings and Photographs

After the Civil War blacks traveled North seeking new homes.

This relaxed shipboard scene contrasts sharply with earlier times.

By the late 1860's blacks sat with whites on juries.

But in Philadelphia blacks were still expelled from railway cars.

Harriet Tubman in a photo made about 1870. She died in 1913.

chapter ten

Although 1859 found the North and South enmeshed in power politics, William Still's people—the pawns—occupied his interests to a marked degree. That year brought no decline in the steady flow of fugitives to the Committee seeking a passage to Canada.

Indeed, on the Fourth of July, while all was hilarity and rejoicing, a party of slaves made off from the eastern shore in spite of safeguards instituted the previous year to prevent an increase in runaways. One of the slaves—Miles Robertson—who ran away from the same neighborhood where the Reverend Samuel Green had been convicted for having a copy of *Uncle Tom's Cabin,* made his way successfully into Pennsylvania.

He had been the slave of Mrs. Roberts, a widow, living in York County, Virginia. But he did not live with her because he was hired out in the city of Richmond. While indentured he enjoyed a fair amount of leisure that he devoted to playing the banjo. He even, in time, became quite gifted on this instrument. Yet he craved liberty, not musical proficiency. Therefore, his thoughts wandered over Mason and Dixon's line long before he did.

187

He was twenty-two and very manly in appearance, with a mind alive with determination.

The news that he was about to be sold made him resolve to escape via the Underground Railroad. Without as much as a word of farewell to his mother, brother, and sisters who were also slaves, he contacted an agent who communicated his wishes to a colored woman working as cook and chambermaid on one of the Philadelphia and Richmond steamers. She arranged to get him a safe berth in one of the closets where the pots and pans and other cooking utensils belonged.

After a rough ordeal, he found himself in the presence of antislavery men in Philadelphia. But Boston had been his goal. Therefore, he paused only a short while before starting for that Northern city, where he found liberty as sweet as he had imagined.

Soon he found work in a hotel where he became a waiter. In his spare time he learned to read and write as well as working in the local churches where members of his race met. He spent four years under the shadow of Bunker Hill, in Charlestown, Massachusetts—a section of Boston—and at the end of this time he invested his savings in a business with two young friends in Philadelphia. Since they were all first-class waiters, understanding the catering business, they decided to open a large dining salon.

Shortly afterward, Miles ran into the ugliness of racial prejudice in the City of Brotherly Love. It happened on the passenger cars.

One evening, at the corner of Fourth and Walnut streets, Miles and two other young men—Wallace and Marshall—entered the cars in a most orderly manner and took their seats. The conductor ordered them to move to the front platform, but they refused to budge. He stopped the cars and ordered them out. This did no good. He read rules to these polite, well-dressed passengers, stating that they had to sit on the front platform. When they refused to move, he called the police, who arrived and arrested all three black men. But Miles did not yield his seat without a struggle. In fact, when he was forcibly pulled from the car he resisted so vehemently that several window lights in the car were broken.

The police came out in force and marched their prisoners to the police station at the corner of Fifth and Chestnut streets, where they were locked up to await further investigation. The prisoners thought they were back in "Old Virginny."

Miles gritted his teeth and grew indignant while he pondered what to do. The prejudice against which he had struggled now controlled all the city car lines in Philadelphia.

He and his companions were willing to suffer for the sake of a principle, but the dirt, filth, and cold as well as the wretchedness of the quarters in which they were compelled to spend the night and the following day—Sunday— shook them somewhat. In addition, Miles worried about his young wife who, he felt, would be very much upset by the whole situation. It was in desperation, therefore, that he called upon William Still, the black man who had befriended him when he arrived at the Anti-slavery office as a fugitive. Still had become known as the person to send for when a member of his race faced trouble of any kind.

Quickly, on hearing of the former slave's unfortunate position, Still sought the Alderman's boardinghouse, since he was the official to accept bail money for the release of the incarcerated blacks. He rushed from the boardinghouse to the fire-engine house and to all the other places he sup-

189

posed the Alderman might be found. But Still soon realized that in his effort to post bail money he was being sent on a wild-goose chase. When he returned to the Alderman's the third time, he found the Alderman had been in bed all evening. Since the night was stormy, William Still and his friend who had accompanied him found it difficult not to believe they had been deliberately deceived.

The officials finally accepted the offer to go bail for all the prisoners and they were released.

But Miles was not satisfied. He had breathed the free air of Massachusetts for four years, and being a man of high spirits, was determined to test further the prejudice on the cars. He was out with his wife on a cold night when a deep snow covered the pavements. He put his wife, who was very fair, on the car at the corner of Third and Pine. Then he walked to the corner of Fourth and Pine where he stepped into the car and took a seat.

The conductor ordered him out on the grounds that his skin was black.

"How is it my wife is in the car?" asked Miles.

All eyes turned to see who his wife was. By this time the car was stopped by a wrathful conductor. He did not, however, lay violent hands upon Miles. This was due, in part, to a late decision in court which taught the police that they had no right to interfere unless the peace was actually interrupted. In order to get rid of the individual, the car was run off the tracks, forcing the shivering passengers to leave it, as though flying from a plague—all except Miles, his wife, and another colored man who boarded with him. Then the conductor hoisted all the windows, took out the cushions, and unhitched the horses.

Enraged, Miles stood firm. He and the other two oc-

190

cupants of the horseless car which was being aired so thoroughly remained in it for awhile. Soon they, too, forsook it.

Prior to this event, Miles had worked to save in order to buy a comfortable brick house with the idea of remaining in Philadelphia. But his ill treatment on the cars reminded him so vividly of his former life as a slave that he decided to place his property on the market—including his business —and to return to Boston to live.

He received an offer, accepted it, and pulled up stakes. In a place called Chelsea, near Boston, he began a kerosene business and bought a beautiful home.

But the episode inspired William Still to step up his campaign in Philadelphia for the right of his people to ride on the cars with greater freedom. He had been complaining of this discrimination long before the Robertson case. In fact, during the summer of 1859, William Still—except for a brief visit to Boston to see how the Underground Railroad passengers fared there—had started to devote his energies to securing equal rights for black citizens on the city railroad cars. In a carefully thought out offensive, Still wrote a letter to the editor of the *North American and United States Gazette:*

Colored People and the Cars

Sir:

As a colored man, and constant reader of your paper, allow me a brief corner in your columns to make a few remarks on the sore grievance of genteel people in being excluded from the city passenger railroad cars, except they choose to "stand on the front platform with the driver."

However long the distance they may have to go, or great their hurry—however unwell or aged, genteel or neatly at-

191

tired—however hot, cold or stormy the weather—however few in the cars, as the masses of colored people now understand it, they are unceremoniously excluded.

Of course my own humble opinion will weigh but little with yourself and readers (being as I am, of the proscribed class) as to whether it is reasonable or unreasonable, just or unjust—as to whether it is a loss or a gain to railroad companies, thus to exclude colored people. Nevertheless, pardon me for saying that this severe proscription, for some unaccountable reason, is carried to an extent in Philadelphia unparalleled in any of the leading cities of this Union. This is not imagination or exaggerated assertion.

In New Orleans, colored people—slaves as well as free—ride in all the city cars and omnibuses. In Cincinnati, colored women are accommodated in the city omnibuses, but colored men are proscribed to a certain extent. In Chicago, it may be safely said that not the slightest proscription exists in the public conveyances of that flourishing city. In New York, Brooklyn, etc. (except in one or two of the New York City passenger lines) there is not the slightest barrier to any persons riding, on account of complexion. There is no obstruction in the way of colored people riding in any of the Boston cars or omnibuses.

I need not allude to the cities of minor importance, whether favorable or unfavorable, North or South. Sufficient are the facts in the examples of the cities already alluded to, to make it a very painfully serious inquiry with intelligent colored people, why it is so in Philadelphia, the city of "Brotherly Love," so noted as the bulwark of the "Religious Society of Friends, commonly called Quakers," so noted as one of the leading cities in the Union, in great religious and benevolent enterprises, so pre-eminently favorable to elevating the heathen in Africa, while forgetful of those in their very precincts—those who are taxed to support the very highways that they are rejected from.

192

But, doubtless, on a hurried consideration of the claims of the colored people, serious objections would be found by railroad boards and others, under the erroneous impressions that the vicinity of St. Mary, Bedford, Seventh, and Lombard Streets, etc. furnishes a sample of the great body of colored people residing in Philadelphia.

I beg, Mr. Editor, to respectfully add, that the inhabitants of this ill-fated region are by no means a fair sample of the twenty thousand colored people of Philadelphia. The gulf between this degraded class and the great mass of industrious colored people, is well nigh as marked as was the gulf between Dives and Lazarus, in the parable; as I shall attempt to demonstrate here, besides volunteering further to prove, by ocular testimony, if any of your readers choose to condescend to accompany me to parts and places where the decent portions of colored people reside; to the eighteen or twenty colored churches, with their Sabbath Schools, to at least twenty day schools, of a public and private character; to the dozens of beneficial societies, united for the mutual support of their sick and disabled members; to the neat and genteelly furnished three-story brick houses, owned, occupied, and paid taxes for, almost entirely by colored people—on Rodman Street, Ronaldson Street, and Washington Street; to observe the extent of valuable property owned on South and Lombard Streets (in the most respectable part of these streets); to examine some of the stores (they may not be large) kept by colored men (of which more will be said presently); to pass those living in respectable houses here, houses alone worth from five to ten thousand dollars; likewise leaving out the many in various other parts of the city, where industrious, sober and decent people live and own considerable real estate. I think abundant evidence may be found in the directions alluded to, to convince the most prejudiced against the colored man, that he is by no means so sadly degraded and miserably poor as the public has gen-

193

erally been led to suppose, from all that has been said of him in connection with the degraded localities alluded to before.

But what avails all this? Why further add in this direction? I fear you will say Mr. Editor. Suppose Stephen Smith, who is reputed to be worth a quarter of a million dollars, with his tens of thousands of dollars invested in bank stocks, etc. etc., having for so many years been well known among business men as an extensive lumber and coal merchant, dealer in real estate, etc., with taxes amounting to nearly $2,000 per annum to pay, should enter a car; still being colored, he would justly be assigned the "front platform," to stand up by the driver.

Again, suppose Miss Greenfield (The Black Swan) wished to enjoy a ride to Fairmount, never mind, she must stand on the "front platform" by the driver too. The fact that her extraordinary acquirements as a vocalist have won for her the very highest distinction both in this country and Europe, does actually weigh nothing when entering a City Passenger Railroad car—the front platform is the place for all that the Creator chose to make with a dark skin.

But I will now relieve your patience, trusting ere long, decent colored men and women will find the same privilege in the City Passenger Railroad cars of Philadelphia that are extended to colored men and women in other cities.

W. S.

Phila. Aug. 30, 1859

Still's letter attracted a good deal of attention and comment. Almost every antislavery paper in the country commended him on the timeliness of the article. But these people knew as well as he that the fight against discrimination aimed at black people was just beginning. It would be long and tough—almost as long and tough as the one in

194

which they were at the moment so deeply involved. But Still's attention was captured several months later by the attack on Harpers Ferry by John Brown.

Harpers Ferry was in West Virginia, where two rivers—the Shenandoah and the rock-cluttered Potomac—met. Three states could be seen from there. Standing in West Virginia, Maryland lies to the left. And beyond the first mountain ridge on the right lies Virginia.

Six months before his raid on the United States Armory at Harpers Ferry, John Brown had discussed in secret meetings with abolitionists in Boston and Philadelphia a plan to arm as many slaves as he could so they could in turn free others. As the chain reaction of slaves killing their masters caught on, more and more slaves would be free to follow the Allegheny Mountain pathway up to Philadelphia where they would pass through William Still's hands on the Underground Railroad and then to Canada. In the interim, abolitionists stood ready to gather reinforcements of from one- to two-hundred-men units of freed blacks in Canada. They would march down to aid Brown once the insurrection had reached an advanced stage.

The plan was well-formulated to the extent that Brown and one of his men were found with names, dates, and places when they were captured. A massive slave rebellion was in the making now that the abolitionists had given tacit approval to meet fire with fire.

On the night of October 16, 1859—chilly, with a drizzling rain—the fervent man led a band of twenty-two, draped under shawls, to the armory building.

A train moved over the narrow bridge arching the twin-river junction. The raiders forced the conductor to bring the train to a halt.

"Surrender the train!" shouted one of Brown's aides from horseback as frightened passengers stared through the windows in astonishment.

Brown then forced his way into the armory where he handed rifles to the small band of slaves who had come to the place.

"Freedom or death!" shouted one of the insurrectionists.

Alert to what was happening, the conductor of the train pulled the whistle cord, which sent the train ino a forward lurch. It gathered speed and drove into Maryland, where the telegraph flashed the news of the raid to Washington, D.C. They, in turn, notified the militia in Baltimore to prepare troops.

"Slaves are armed!" came the warning.

By now some of Brown's men had moved into neighboring towns to gather slaves.

"Let them free themselves!" the white men shouted.

Due to scanty preparation, not many slaves came forth. Time was ticking by.

Then the militiamen arrived and fired at the insurrectionists.

John Brown dashed into the arsenal for more weapons; but he was caught in the arm by a militiaman's bullet. He fell bleeding to the ground.

By now the Maryland militia was supplemented by the Marines from Washington, D.C., under the command of Robert E. Lee and Army Lieutenant J. E. B. Stuart.

Although John Brown shouted, "Stay with it!" to his men, he soon realized that his poorly executed insurrection was doomed to failure. With his men routed or dead, the wounded leader raised his hands in surrender. He and the remaining men in his party were placed in prison to await trial for attempting to arm the slaves in a revolt.

News of the aborted attempt buzzed throughout the nation, stirring public sentiment both pro and con.

In the North, abolitionists hailed him a "saviour," while in the South he was dismissed as a "fanatic" and "madman."

Frederick Douglass, a slave who had been bought with abolitionists' money, knew about the plot. He had in fact encouraged Brown to carry through the ill-fated plan. Faced now with Brown's failure, Douglass fled to Canada from Rochester, where he waited. He did this advisedly, for the militia found in Brown's shack papers implicating Douglass—and, in fact, William Still.

William Still awaited his fate in Philadelphia, for he expected to face trial for his knowledge in the slave revolt. He hid his records in a loft in a building in the Lebanon Cemetery and vowed to face the dangers aimed at all the abolitionists in the city of Philadelphia. Never before had they felt such tension at the Anti-slavery office. Gloom hung heavy as they prepared to defend their own activities, even as preparations were begun to try Brown and his comrades.

The trial proceeded without delay. Brown was convicted and sentenced to die by hanging. The execution was set for December 2, 1859.

Mr. and Mrs. Still—aware of the suffering to be endured by Brown's wife, daughter, and sons while he awaited execution—invited them to share their home. And when Annie and her mother accepted, the Stills were happy to comfort them.

Part of this time, Frances Ellen Watkins, a dear friend of the Stills who was a poet and writer, joined the Browns as another guest.

She had written the following letter to the grieving woman even before she joined them as a house guest of the Stills:

Farmer Centre, Ohio, Nov. 14th

My Dear Madam:—In an hour like this the common words of sympathy may seem like idle words, and yet I want to say something to you, the noble wife of the hero of the nineteenth century. Belonging to the race your dear husband reached forth his hand to assist, I need not tell you that my sympathies are with you. I thank you for the brave words you have spoken. A republic that produces such a wife and mother may hope for better days. Our heart may grow more hopeful for humanity when it sees the sublime sacrifice it is about to receive from his hands. Not in vain has your dear husband periled all, if the martyrdom of one hero is worth more than the life of a million cowards. From the prison comes forth a shout of triumph over that power whose ethics are robbery of the feeble and oppression of the weak, the trophies of whose chivalry are a plundered cradle and a scourged and bleeding woman. Dear Sister, I thank you for the brave and noble words that you have spoken. Enclosed I send you a few dollars as a token of my gratitude, reverence, and love.

Yours respectfully,
Frances Ellen Watkins

Post Office address: care of William Still, 107 Fifth St., Philadelphia, Penn.

May God, our own God, sustain you in the hour of trial. If there is one thing on earth I can do for you or yours, let me be apprized. I am at your service.

The kind black woman could not forget Brown's comrades, who were also lying in prison under sentences of death. Therefore, she decided to send letters to them to lift their flagging spirits. But the two weeks she had shared under the Still roof produced such a strong emotional involvement with the victims that she decided to write a little later, from Montpelier, where she went to lecture.

Brown went to the gallows stoically.

James McKim and other friends stood at the side of the convicted man to the end. The abolitionist world mourned! In Boston, Wendell Phillips fought tears! Throughout the North, bells tolled!

Mrs. McKim had accompanied the widow to the scene. They, and the Honorable Hector Tyndale, of Philadelphia prominence, rode in the back of the train with the coffin.

The party was met at the railroad station in Philadelphia by a group of free colored people. The route they traveled was mobbed by the famous as well as the little-known antislavery sympathizers. They came to pay homage to the hero. With tears brimming their eyes, they watched the train move north for the burial.

In Philadelphia, the Reverend William H. Furness took part in the public meeting held on the day of John Brown's execution, offering prayers to the heroic soul that was passing away then. And when the train passed through Philadelphia, he and two or three others went to the railroad station to receive the martyr's body. He feared, all the while, that his church would be the first to receive the brunt of slavery's wrath.

The funeral party arrived in New York. Wendell Phillips, Boston's great orator in antislavery matters, joined James McKim, and the others, and they passed on through North Elba, Troy, Rutland, Westport, Rochester, Syracuse, and Fitchburg with crowds lined along the way, mourning.

Cleveland was draped in black. In Boston, Tremont Temple was thronged by those wishing to pay homage to Brown's memory. Wendell Phillips delivered an oration as

199

the body was lowered into the ground in the Adirondacks. It was an oration to celebrate the death of the martyr who had made the first vain effort to strike the chains from the body of the slave!

Yet instead of demoralizing the ranks devoted to the abolition of slavery, the recent events served to heighten an interest in the cause, especially throughout the small New England cities and towns. Letters appeared in William Still's mail advising him of collections of money for feeding and clothing fugitives, which came as personal sacrifices made by ladies in sewing circles and church groups. With funds always a problem till now, he read the letters. To those such as the following he replied immediately:

Ellington, Chautauqua Co., N. Y.
December 7th, 1859

Mr. Still:—Dear Sir:—Yours of the 29th, was duly and gratefully received, although the greater portion of your epistle, of a necessity, portrayed the darker side of the picture, yet we have great reason to be thankful for the growing interest there is for the cause throughout the free States, for it certainly is on the increase, even in our own locality. There are those who, five years since, were (ashamed, must I say it!) to bear the appellation of "Anti-Slavery," who can now manfully bear the one then still more repellant of "Abolitionist." All this we wish to feel thankful for, and wish their number may never grow less.

The excitement relative to the heroic John Brown, now in his grave, has affected the whole North, or at least everyone who has a heart in his breast, particularly this portion of the State, which is so decidedly Anti-slavery.

At the meeting of our Society, to-day, at which your letter was read, it was thought best that I should reply to it, a request with which I cheerfully comply. We would like to hear

200

from you, and learn the directions to be given to our box, which will be ready to send as soon as we can hear from you. Please give us all necessary information, and Oblige our Society.

You have the kind wishes and prayers of all the members, and you may be the instrument of doing much good to those in bonds, and may God speed the time when every yoke shall be broken, and let the oppressed go free.

Yours truly,
Mrs. D. Brooks

William Still welcomed the aid that sympathizers such as Mrs. Brooks sent. And fugitives continued to pour over Mason and Dixon's line into the city of Philadelphia. The winter of 1860 found the shivering wretches placing heavy demands on the facilities at the Anti-slavery office. If donations such as those offered by Mrs. Brooks had not been forthcoming, the Committee would scarcely have met the needs of the fugitives.

She wrote a letter in January, 1861, in which she listed the articles of clothing she was forwarding to Still. It mentioned bed quilts, cotton socks, stockings, woolen socks, men's shirts, as well as chemises, pants and overalls, pillow cases and calico aprons, sunbonnets and aprons, and finally, capes and shawls.

Boxes of clothing and supplies were gratefully accepted by the Committee members in Philadelphia. But funds were slow in arriving. Although stockholders managed to secure funds for various other Underground Railroad stations throughout the North, for some unknown reason money was rarely sent to the Vigilance Committee in Philadelphia.

But words of encouragement were received with regularity by William Still from abolitionists as far away as England. These letters carried the opinions of antislavery men such as the Honorable George Thompson, close friend of James McKim, the Duke of Argyll, John Stuart Mill, and William Wilberforce.

Anna H. Richardson—an active member of the Great Britain Abolitionist circle, informed him that they were quite aware of the encroachment of the proslavery elements in America upon the states of the North.

She enclosed a letter dated May 25, 1860, from Newport, which read:

I am glad to tell you we feel it a great victory over the slave power to be able to rise again from our ruins, and in the face of slave-owning despots denounce their inhumanity and their sins. I trust that Almighty God will continue to be with me and my dear family in this good work.

You cannot but see, I think, by the Southern press, that the slave-holders begin to fear and tremble for the safety of their "peculiar institution." The death of John Brown is yet to be atoned for, by the slave-holding Oligarchy. His undying spirit haunts them by day and by night, and in the midst of their voluptuous enjoyments, the very thought of John Brown chills their souls and poisons their pleasures. Their tarring and feathering of good citizens; their riding them upon rails; and ducking them in dirty ponds; their destruction of liberty presses, and the hanging of John Brown and his friends, to intimidate men from the advocacy of freedom, will all come tumbling down upon their own heads as a just retribution for their outrageous brutality. Only let us persevere, and oppressed humanity, bent in timid silence throughout the South, will rise and throw off the yoke of Slavery, and rejoice in beholding itself *FREE!"*

Mrs. Richardson wrote about the Bereans—inhabitants of a village in Kentucky, where Christian men and women pursued useful labors during the 1850's. Holding strong antislavery sentiments, they ran a farm and sawmill and established a flourishing school. After the John Brown episode, sixty-two armed Kentuckians rode on horseback to their cottage doors informing them to leave the state in ten days' time or be expelled forcibly. The community members were aware that pleading was in vain. Therefore, they gathered their belongings and fled to Ohio in only three days.

When one of the exiles returned to Kentucky, an outbreak of popular feeling resulted in mob violence, which led to the burning of his sawmill.

John G. Fee—one of the leaders of the Bereans who himself was a former slaveholder—speaking in the role of minister of the gospel which he now espoused, said: "The land was poor, but the situation beautiful, with good water, and a favorable location, in some respects. We could have had locations more fertile and more easy of access, but more exposed to the slave-power. It was five miles from a turnpike road, with quite a population around it for a slave-State."

The articulate English lady discussed the subject of Free Produce in her letter to William Still. She stated that if enough members of the English Anti-slavery Society were prepared to make the sacrifice—out of conscience—not to buy slave-produce, the institution of slavery would be short-lived.

She spoke of the earnest lectures in Newcastle by M. R. Delaney, the black man from America. He spoke of non-slave produce. In fact, at the time she wrote, he was in West Africa where he longed to establish a colony of black people who would work to put down the abominable slave trade and cultivate free cotton and other tropical produce.

203

She described his efforts to gain the confidence of "The African Aid Society" in London, who assisted him with funds.

She also wrote about cotton-growing in Jamaica under the magistrate of Stephen Bourne. Still read the quotes from this entrepreneur:

Our schemes embrace more than meets the eye, and to illustrate this, I send a map (with prospectus) of the proposed estate, by which you will see that we reckon on obtaining cotton by free labor and by mechanical agency from Jamaica, at a price so far below that at which it can be produced by slave labor, that if we succeed, we shall put an end to the whole system, as no one will be able to afford to carry it on in competition with free labor produce. . . .

Jamaica is much nearer and easier of access for fugitives from Cuba and Porto Rico, than Canada is from Georgia, Virginia, or Louisiana. If, therefore, we can offer them an asylum and profitable employment on the estate, we shall open up a new Underground Rail Road, or rather enable the slaves to escape from Cuba by getting into a boat, and in one night finding their way to Freedom. . . .

There is no doubt they could do this at much less risk than slaves now incur, in order to obtain liberty in America.

The proposed estate in Jamaica consists of about one thousand acres. The shares in this company are £ 10 each— £ 1 to be called up immediately and the rest by installments. The liability is limited. Full information may be obtained by addressing Stephen Bourne, Esq., 55 Charing Cross, London, or the Secretary of the "Jamaica Cotton-growing Company," C. W. Streatfield, Esq. We rejoice to see that this new company is being supported not only by benevolent philanthropists and capitalists in London, but by experienced Manchester manufacturers; among the rest by the excellent

Thomas Clegg, so well known for his persevering efforts in West Africa, and by Thomas Bazley, M. P. for Manchester, and a most expensive cotton spinner. Their mills would alone consume the cotton from all three such estates as that which it is proposed to cultivate. There is abundant room, therefore, for cultivation of cotton by the emancipated freeholders.

Then Still read a letter dated December 28, 1860, from Mrs. Richardson, in which she counseled him and the Committee members to watch out for their personal safety:

"I think, dear friend, thou shouldst be careful not to be about alone, particularly in the evening. . . .

"Would it not be well to make a habit, in the evening in particular, of you, who are marked men, going about in little companies? Wicked men are generally cowards; and I think I would hesitate more to do a bad act in the presence of observers."

The possibility of violence in Philadelphia had occurred to William Still. In fact, it was no secret that he and his colleagues had for a long time expected this city to be the first arena in the bloody contest none doubted was coming. In the words of Dr. Furness in his sermon on John Brown: "Out of the grim cloud that hangs over the South, a bolt has darted, and blood has flowed, and the place where the lightning has struck is wild with fear."

The sermon he preached in December, 1860, printed in the Boston *Atlas,* prophesied:

But the trouble cannot be escaped. It must come. But we can put it off. By annihilating free speech; by forbidding the utterance of a word in the pulpit and by the press; for the rights of man; by hurling back into the jaws of oppression, the fugitive gasping for his sacred liberty; by recognizing the

205

right of one man to buy and sell other men; by spreading the blasting curse of despotism over the whole soil of the nation, you may allay the brutal frenzy of a handful of southern slave-masters.

You may win back the cotton states to cease from threatening you with secession, and to plant their feet upon your necks, and so evade the trouble that now menaces us. Then you may live on the few years that are left you, and perhaps —it is not certain—we may be permitted to make a little more money and die in our beds. But, no friends, I am mistaken. We cannot put the trouble off! Or we put it off in its present shape, only that it may take another more terrible form. . . .

Death is the worst that can befall us, if so, be that we are faithful to the right. It is a solemn and fearful thing to die, my friends, and the dying hour is not far distant from the youngest of us. To many, only a few brief years remain. And for the sake of these few and uncertain years, shall we push off this present trouble upon our children, who have to stay here a little longer? . . .

And now in these times of great trouble which have come upon us, we have a peculiar and special opportunity of testifying our fidelity and of enjoying a full experience of its powers to support us. We may gather from this trouble, a sweetness that shall take away from all suffering its bitterness. We may kindle the light in our bosoms, which shall make death come to us as a radiant angel.

Four months after this sermon was delivered, on the 28th of April, 1861, Fort Sumter, South Carolina, was fired upon. The North burst into flames! People of all denominations flocked to Dr. Furness' church to hear his powerful sermon: "The long agony is over!"

It was the *Te Deum* of a lifetime for the abolitionists.

chapter eleven

The year 1861 found the United States engaged in a bloody civil war. The Pennsylvania Anti-slavery Society postponed its annual meeting—for the first time since it had been formed.

Although black people were running away from their masters in ever increasing numbers, many slaves waited on the plantations throughout the South for "Massa Lincoln to free them." Harriet Tubman had delivered the last arrivals to William Still's office in Philadelphia, although he had warned her not to risk returning to the South.

But as the months wore on, the expectation that Lincoln would soon free the slaves receded, and Still turned his attention again to problems of discrimination in Philadelphia.

That same year, William Still, as a member of the Executive Committee of the Anti-slavery Society, drew up a petition under the auspices of its Social, Civil, and Statistical Association in favor of equal rights for the black man while riding the railway passenger cars. This association, of which Still was Chairman, was founded to collect facts about black people in order to dispel racial prejudice. It tried to counteract the popular belief in the so-called inferiority of the former slaves by presenting new evidence. In addition, it secured famous lecturers, both black and white, to speak about citizenship responsibilities, race, and human relations. In essence, its purpose was to strike at the roots of racial prejudice.

William Still, together with his long-time friends— Stephen M. Smith, I. C. Wears, and Reverend J. C. Gibbs —was able to get at least three hundred and sixty of Philadelphia's most prominent white citizens to sign the petition. It was presented at the monthly meeting of the Board of Presidents of the City Passenger Railway Cars. The president of the Chestnut and Walnut Street Road at first relented; then, after more talk on the subject, decided to postpone a final decision until the next meeting of the Board.

But William Still continued to press. He sent a letter dated December 15, 1863, to the Philadelphia *Press* in which he described an unpleasant experience he had endured as a black man riding the cars: the conductor had forced him to ride on the platform, in the snow, because of his color, and had charged him full fare. His letter declared: "Nowhere in Christendom could I find a better example of Judge Taney's decision of the Dred Scott case which declared that 'a black man has no rights which white men are bound to respect' when it came to his right to ride freely on the cars in Philadelphia."

To his surprise, the letter drew interest and comment in the press even outside the United States. It appeared in the London *Times*.

In the winter of 1862, the feeling grew that the emancipation of the slaves was imminent. James McKim called a meeting of citizens to consider and provide for the needs of the thousands of slaves who might suddenly be liberated. And in January, 1863, came the Emancipation Proclamation! The slaves were free!

Words such as these from William Whipper, a former Underground Railroad conductor, expressed the sentiments of his many colleagues:

"Now the slaves are emancipated . . . after struggling for existence, freedom, and manhood—I feel thankful for having had the glorious privilege of laboring with others for the redemption of my race from oppression and thraldom; and I would prefer to be penniless in the streets rather than have withheld a single hour's labor or a dollar from the sacred cause of liberty, justice, and humanity."

James McKim began to feel that the usefulness of the Anti-slavery Society was over, and he turned his attention toward helping the newly freed slaves. He traveled extensively in the South as well as in the North, where he organized public sentiment in their behalf.

Although William Still was anxious to return to battle with the railway car presidents, other more pressing duties were forced upon him. James McKim offered him the job of post sutler in the colored soldiers' camp. This was a position dealing with supplying food to the commissary. At first he hesitated, then he accepted, although it meant taking time from his lucrative coal business.

But Still could not forget his crusade for equal rights for his race on the cars. He and others continued the struggle by personal visits, direct appeals, and interviews. But now these appeals were strengthened by the presence of black soldiers who were fighting in the Union ranks.

Soon the abolitionists joined forces with Still in an out and out campaign to fight for equal rights for black passenger-car riders. Alfred H. Love, one of the members of the Anti-slavery Society, proposed a meeting for September 28. A bill had been passed by one House of the Pennsylvania legislature to remove all restrictions on the cars due to race. The members of the car committee wrote letters discussing their views to several candidates for the legislature, the Mayoralty, and the District Attorney. The candidates who replied favorably and promptly regarding this cause received their votes and were elected by a large majority.

They kept up the pressure. And progress was being made. The following circular from the car committee to the Board of Presidents of the City Passenger Railway Cars stated:

> Since our petition was first presented New York has removed proscription from all the city passenger cars—although the rules of her roads, long before this final change, carried colored people, generally without proscription, except two roads. In these exceptional cases they could ride in cars especially designated by the words, "Colored people are allowed, etc."
>
> Can it be possible that there is more prejudice and less humanity in Philadelphia than in New York? We cannot think so. . . .
>
> In conclusion, permit us to express the earnest hope that our efforts this time will meet with a more favorable result than before, and that not many weeks or months shall pass ere such changes will be made as shall remove the cause of complaint for the future.
>
> Respectfully yours,
> Wm. Still
> Isaiah C. Wears ⎬ Committee
> S. M. Smith
> J. C. Gibbs

210

To further the cause, Still, along with James McKim, arranged to hold a meeting at Concert Hall to be attended by many of the prominent men who had signed the petition. At the meeting resolutions were adopted unanimously, opposing the exclusion of blacks. A committee, too, was appointed to present each of the presidents with a copy of these resolutions.

Six years had passed since a bill had been introduced in the Pennsylvania legislature to prohibit discrimination on the cars. But finally success came! On March 18th, 1867, a bill was passed in the House of Representatives!

Yet at this, their moment of triumph, black people in Philadelphia became openly critical of William Still. Many ordinary black citizens feared the power he was able to wield. Some were envious of his financial success. At any rate, Still became the butt of their frustrated feelings. They turned on him and some even spread the word not to buy his coal.

In order to silence these troublemakers, William Still decided to declare his position on behalf of the black man. He wrote a pamphlet which he called "A Brief Narrative of the Struggle for the Rights of the Colored People of Philadelphia in the City Railway Cars; and a Defence of William Still, Relating to His Agency Touching the Passage of the Late Bill."

This caption appeared on the front, and on the back was an advertisement for his coal, with comments he had taken from two Philadelphia newspapers.

> Coal Under Cover!
>   Wm. Still,
> Dealer In
> Lehigh and Schuylkill Coal,

Office and Yard
Nos. 1216, 1218, and 1220 Washington Avenue
Above 12th Street, South Side,
Philadelphia.
Orders received at 413 Lombard Street.

Deserving of Compliment—Among our advertisers is one who has already made himself most deservedly popular by his earnest and well-directed efforts for the elevation of his race. We refer to Mr. Wm. Still. He was one of the prime movers amongst the colored people of this city to secure for themselves proper means of social advancement, and on many occasions he had shown a most proper spirit of liberality. In his business transactions he has won a deservedly high reputation for integrity and promptness, and his coal-yard on Washington Avenue is an evidence of the success with which he has met. *North American and United States Gazette,* February 9th, 1867.

A Good Place to Get Coal.—Mr. Wm. Still has now the finest coal-yard on Washington Avenue, fitted up by himself with an office, a stable, a car-track, and all the appurtenances and needs of a first-class coal depot. Everything seems to be constructed in the most substantial manner, wearing a neat, attractive appearance. His coal is of good quality, and is furnished to dealers on liberal terms.

Despite all the trouble it had brought, William Still was relieved that the passenger car episode had ended in success.

Now he turned to several other welfare projects for the benefit of his people. The Pennsylvania Anti-slavery Society, in the early postwar era, continued to fight for the rights of the black man. They donated two hundred dollars to the Home for Aged and Infirm Colored Persons. Two hundred more went to spread information about the Fifteenth Amendment, which had not been ratified at the time. Further attempts were made to gain more political power for blacks in the State of Pennsylvania.

So many projects left William Still little time for purely social affairs. But just after the close of the war, out of gratitude and admiration, he entertained William Lloyd Garrison in his home as a guest of honor. Many abolitionists came. But it did not end there. When the "Executive Committee of the National Testimonial to William Lloyd Garrison," headed by John A. Andrews of Massachusetts, was making an effort to raise a purse of fifty thousand dollars, unknown to Mr. Garrison, William Still contributed one hundred dollars.

Aware that its usefulness was ending, the Pennsylvania Anti-slavery Society proposed and unanimously passed the following resolution in May, 1871:

> *Whereas,* The position of William Still in the Vigilance Committee connected with the "Underground Rail Road," as its corresponding secretary, and chairman of its acting sub-committee, gave him peculiar facilities for collecting interesting facts pertaining to this branch of the anti-slavery service; therefore
>
> *Resolved,* That the Pennsylvania Anti-slavery Society request him to compile and publish his personal reminiscences and experiences relating to the "Underground Rail Road."

Still complied willingly. As he began to assemble the data he needed to write the book, he heard from his brother James, in Medford, New Jersey. James requested a family reunion at his house. William was happy to accept because he had not seen James since their brother Peter's death, which had occurred not too many years after he settled on a small farm near his people.

At the appointed time, William and his wife, Letitia,

213

crossed the Delaware River on the ferry and took a stage out into the country where his brother, now a well-to-do doctor, had a lovely home about twenty-five miles from Camden. When they arrived and knocked at the door of the house, it was opened with the warm greeting of the black doctor, "William—and Letitia! Come in! Come in!"

They entered the comfortably furnished living room dominated by a warm glowing hearth. Moving about the large room were the remaining children of Levin and Charity Still, former slaves. Now only seven remained: Mahalah Thompson and her husband, and the widowed Kitturah Willmore—both born in slavery; Samuel, the first freeborn son; Mary Still, a spinster; Charles Still, a bachelor; James and his wife Henrietta.

They broke open a bottle of aged wine and drank a toast to their health.

The conversation ran to the events of James's children. His oldest son, James, Jr., now attended the Harvard School of Medicine in Boston, where he was busy preparing a thesis on hay fever and hay asthma for his impending graduation. His other children were Joseph, William, Eliza Ann, Emmaretta, Angelina, and Lucretia.

James reminisced about his own early lack of education. But his powers to heal brought him more patients than he could care for. Over the years he had earned money by working all hours of the night. With this money he bought property on which there was a building he used for a "hospital." Soon money accumulated for the addition of more land. With his land, buildings, wagon and pair, and cash, he was a wealthy man. He owned nearly all the northeast corner of the Crossroads in Medford. His property had a half mile of frontage on the main road. Adjacent to his house stood a laboratory for the preparation of his medicine

214

—the salves and herb prescriptions he used for his miraculous cure of "skin cancer."

It was a familiar sight to see him drive to church on Sunday in the carriage with his wife and elegantly dressed daughters. No finer looking family lived in Medford Township.

When he told his sisters and brothers of the old tavern-keeper who owned most of the land before he bought it, he described the way he was ridiculed: "I'd like to have a bunch of nigger bones to hang from the rafters," the white man had said when he anticipated Still would want to buy his land. Yet Still managed to buy him out.

He had partially rebuilt the tavern property by adding a forty-foot front section and enlarging the building. Then he made it three stories high. He rented out the structure under the name of "Still's Hotel." He used the building from time to time as a hospital to accommodate the large number of patients who came to him to be cured. His reputation grew. The hour was never too late, nor the distance too far for the friendly old doctor to travel to the bedside of the sick or afflicted.

When William heard that his nephew in Boston was soon to intern at the Massachusetts General Hospital there, he marveled that he and his brother had been so fortunate in life, considering the dim prospects they faced as youths.

The hour grew late, and William parted from his beloved family reluctantly. But he had work to do in Philadelphia. The few pleasant moments they had shared lingered in his mind all the way home. The thought occurred to him that he might never see his people again.

Yet even on his way home, his thoughts were of the book he was about to write. The slave was to be the hero, that much he was sure of. No matter what some of the freed blacks thought of him and his prominence now, his thoughts always dwelt on the early days when the penniless bondsmen stole over the border seeking food and shelter on the way to Canada. William Still's attitude had not changed. He loved them very dearly now as before.

In 1871 a strike of coal miners provided the leisure which enabled him to devote more time to writing the book. Dr. Caroline Still, his oldest child, a graduate of Oberlin College, in Ohio, helped him tremendously. In 1872 the large book was published by Porter and Coates—antislavery printers. The first edition sold ten thousand copies, by private subscription. A second printing was prepared for publication at a later date. It was distributed mainly to antislavery men and women intimately involved in the abolition movement in Philadelphia, although some copies went to abolitionists in other cities.

With this monumental task behind him, William Still was free to work for better education for his people. He traveled to Washington, D.C., and cities in the border states armed with letters of introduction from prominent antislavery men in Philadelphia. In reviewing the facilities open to the black man, he gained a better idea of what had to be done to improve their lot.

Now the political arena captured his interest. At the June 27th meeting of the Anti-slavery Society in 1872, the matter of constitutional amendments in Pennsylvania were evaluated. A committee was formed. William Still, Alfred H. Love, and a Mr. Warringer were selected to head it. In its report on November 11, they proposed the following changes in the Constitution:

"Art. 1, Sect. 25. Amend by inserting after the word 'corporators' at the end of the first clause or period 'and no corporation shall be established within this Commonwealth which shall make any discrimination in the exercise of its public provisions or franchise against any citizen of the United States on account of color.'

"Add as a new section to Art. 2, Sect. 27. 'No public hotel or tavern and no theatre or other place of public use.' "

It was well known that the Still family was a happy one. He and his wife enjoyed their children and, because of their relative prosperity, were able to give them a good education. Therefore, when the opportunity was presented to Still to join the board of trustees of several philanthropic organizations for those less fortunate, he readily accepted. One was the Home for Destitute Children, and another was called the Shelter, a home for children at 53rd Street near Woodlyn Avenue in Philadelphia. He became a Trustee at Storer College—a school for black students, at Harpers Ferry, West Virginia.

He encouraged black authors such as William Wells Brown and Frances Ellen Watkins, who had married a man named Harper and had written a book, *Sketches of Southern Life.* When Wells, a former slave, produced a book called *The Black Man,* Still praised his efforts.

His attempts to promote the written word were not confined to members of his own race. At the end of the war several able men who had worked in the abolition movement approached him about the establishment of a newspaper which would present an impartial opinion on politics, science, literature, and art.

One hundred thousand dollars was thought sufficient to establish stock. Mr. Still subscribed one thousand of this amount and the paper appeared as "The Nation." It was edited by Edward Godkin, and "in the course of a few years set a new standard of free and intelligent criticism of public affairs."

Now that the war was over, citizenship rights for the freed slave occupied the thoughts of liberals. But others, like Mr. Thomas Webster, considered the possibility of black economic advancement. He proposed that he and Still establish a bank for blacks to invest in which would be composed of equal numbers of whites and blacks.

At first Still was elated. He did know several prominent black men who, he was quite certain, would be only too glad to become involved. Then he had second thoughts. What he needed first, he decided, was more information about such a project. Shortly afterward, he asked twenty-five black men to meet with a group of white men. They formed a committee to investigate the chances for success. William Still was made Chairman. At a meeting held at Stephen M. Smith's house, John Torrey, the President of the Corn Exchange Bank, informed the committee members about all facets of banking. He discussed the duties of a director, the qualities necessary for efficient management, the importance of capable and honest clerical workers, all in the most minute detail. Then he spoke about training, experience, and talent. They listened intently.

But an adverse report on the project was adopted. Granting all arguments that the bank would benefit his race—if established on a firm foundation—Still foresaw a lack of black men who, at that time, had sufficiently well-developed business skills to manage such an undertaking successfully.

In other words, he thought that the "scheme was in advance of the talent essential to its success." His report states that it was "in substance worthy as to conception, plausible as to argument, but inopportune as to time."

The bank plan was abandoned.

But there were many more struggles and projects to occupy the energies of William Still. Since the Republican Party had been the party of Lincoln, many black people swore loyalty to it. In the election for Mayor in 1874, W. S. Stokely, the Republican, and A. K. McClure, the Democrat, running from the People's Party, were the candidates. Few doubted that blacks would vote Republican.

William Still declared the Democrat the better man. A great wave of protest came from the mass of black people. His popularity fell rapidly. Again, some attempted to hurt his coal business by urging other blacks not to buy from him. Some said his business had grown because he consorted with those in politics who had helped him, and that he was repaying political debts by telling blacks how to vote. It was true that his coal business had become lucrative, but this was due to his business acumen. He had established a reputation for being a sound merchant. It was also true that he had, from time to time, traveled with his friends to the coal-producing regions of Pennsylvania for business as well as pleasure, and had received the usual letters asking him to become a member of the Philadelphia Board of Trade.

Still had accepted, and was notified that he had been approved unanimously.

This high degree of prominence brought even more criticism! Threats were made to burn down his coal-yard! Still feared they were about to lynch him. If it had not been for the intervention of the police, who protected him at his home, they might have done so.

Then some of these men held an indignation meeting at Liberty Hall. Still and Robert Purvis, his devoted friend from the Anti-slavery office, were accused of being traitors to their principles.

They sent this letter to William Still:

Philadelphia, March 2, 1874

Mr. William Still:
Dear Sir:
In view of the conflicting rumors relative to your vote for Col. A. K. McClure for Mayor, and also in view of the fact of having known, for a long time, of your labors and deep interest in the Anti-slavery cause, and the welfare of our race, we would be pleased to hear a public address from you on the topic of voting, etc., in reply to the charges preferred against you at such time and place, as may suit your convenience.

Still wrote the following reply:

Philadelphia, March 5, 1874

Rev. Theo. Gould
W. C. Banton
Dr. David Rosell
Chaplain Hunter and others

Dear Sirs:
In reply to your kind letter of the 2nd. inst., to the effect that you "would be pleased to hear a public address" from me on the "topic of voting," etc. I would say that it would afford me much satisfaction to make my views publicly known in the manner suggested in Concert Hall on Tuesday evening next, 10th inst. at eight o'clock. Admission free to all.

Yours Respectfully,
William Still

The following excerpt from the Philadelphia *Press* of March 11, 1874, reports the outcome:

220

At Concert Hall assembled last evening, for the purpose of hearing Mr. William Still, one of Philadelphia's most prominent and well-to-do citizens, upon the subject of "Laboring and Voting." The hall was well filled, and the interest as great as ever has been noticed at any other lecture. There were many white people present who have been acquainted with the gentleman for a number of years, and for whom they entertain the greatest respect. . . .

In his stirring address, Still stated frankly that he had no personal political aims. He said he had picked the Democratic candidate on the basis of what he offered his people and not for partisan reasons. Having McClure in office seemed best to him, he repeated, because he would do more for them since they needed help from any source whatsoever. He denied having "played politics." He explained to the assembly that the vote was a vital area in their quest for equality in their new status as citizens.

In the following quotation from one of his articles he explains further:

"For one, I am simple enough to think that the acquisition of knowledge, the pursuit of business enterprises, good trades, and comfortable homes, where a more healthy and reputable existence may be secured, are of infinitely greater consequence than to be in any way connected with Politics."

Over and over again, he declared he felt it ineffective for black people to remain loyal to the Republican Party—simply out of "gratitude." Nor to wait for offices from the Republican Party. "To my mind the work of our elevation, after all, must come mainly through our own exertions and self-reliance. Honest earnest counsel is very much needed on this subject; and hard and steady toiling, economical habits, with a single eye to business, character and integrity,

221

are of incalculable importance as instrumentalities to be employed by every intelligent colored man desiring to see his race elevated."

Gratitude, he continued, belonged to God and to those friends of freedom who endured the greatest sacrifices and sufferings in adhering to the "higher law" and obeying the "commands of Christ to help undo every burden and let the oppressed go free."

He stated his reasons for voting for Mr. McClure. He said he had made up his mind to take his vote away from the "Ring" because of election frauds, high taxes, etc., as well as the strenuous efforts made by this power to defeat the new Constitution. McClure had cooperated with the reformers of Philadelphia; and advocated the Constitutional Convention, attacking defects of the old Constitution and advocating important improvements of the new. He cited the fact that McClure was running for Mayor as a non-partisan on an Independent ticket as one which should have served as an inspiration for colored people—as free-thinking and independent people—to vote according to their honest convictions. It was a self-evident right under a Republican form of government. He called their attention to the fact that many Republicans and prominent abolitionists were against the "Ring" and they, too, had voted for McClure.

As to the "leading colored men" who had addressed the indignation meeting and abused him for "having turned traitor," he recommended that they utilize their energy in some of "those needed fields of industry and reform" to which he had made allusion. Not only did his independent action precipitate a storm of indignation and comment, but it brought to him a rash of letters from all over the United States and from as far as Canada. A survey of several newspapers brought to light some of the more unsavory high-

222

lights of the Philadelphia political "Ring" which resulted in vindicating Still regarding his political attitude.

That he was "more interested in seeking the means to elevate his race than in bowing at the "shrine of politics" is definitely confirmed in light of the facts which follow.

Altogether, William S. Stokely had been elected three times as Mayor, each time on the Republican ticket. He had been approached by William Still, who was anxious to have colored policemen on the Philadelphia force. Still went to the Mayor's office in the company of Reverend Phillips. When the committee of two left his office, the Mayor is reported to have said that he did not need to make any such move because he had the colored vote anyway since colored people always could be counted upon to vote Republican. He had not counted on the fact that the citizens would tire of the "gang rule." They wanted something else.

In this election, the Democrats selected for their candidate, Samuel George King, who had been a member of the Select Council, and who was known for his clear judgment, integrity, and spirit of progress, which gave him a commanding influence which he used for the public good.

William Still and Reverend Phillips made another visit —this time to Mr. King—to see if he would put colored men on the force. He replied that he had no objections and would certainly do so if he was elected. Later he was duly elected Mayor, the first Democrat for many years, and in his inaugural address he took a firm stand in favor of a non-partisan police force.

The result of his promise to William Still is explained as follows:

"The most radical act of Mayor King was the appointment of colored men as members of the police force; as previous to his term no colored man had ever worn the uniform of a policeman of Philadelphia, and his appointment of them (he appointed three) raised such a storm of indignation such as no previous mayor ever encountered; but conscious of the justness of his act, he went on in the even tenor of his way, resting his vindication to time and public opinion."

Plans were now in the making for the Centennial Exhibition of 1876 in Philadelphia. Articles and exhibits of every description were being assembled from all over the country and, for that matter, from all over the world.

For some time William Still had been deeply concerned about how best to represent the thirty thousand or so black citizens of Philadelphia. Since achievements in mechanical science, literature, and the arts had a leading place at the Exhibition, William Still decided to display his book, *The Underground Rail Road*. He exhibited it in various styles of binding, placed in a heavy, handsome glass case where it attracted much attention as one display which showed what progress blacks were making in the arts and industry.

By this time, he had proved that when it came to worthwhile projects, it was hard to match him.

Now he worked with William Whipper, a former black abolitionist, to get a public building where black people could hold meetings. They bought a building on Lombard Street—between Sixth and Seventh, which at one time had been used to house the Institute of Colored Youth. But the company they formed became bankrupt. The other members had died, and Still, in order to recoup his losses, bought it. He renovated the building and made it into a hall which he named Liberty Hall. Soon he held many meetings here. In fact, he held a reception in this hall for the newly appointed black policemen.

The church also claimed his attention. He attended the Central Presbyterian Church and was an officer. Therefore, he conferred with other members about beginning a mission which many had long desired. A mission of this sort was a source of help to those destitute blacks who needed such aid as moral support, or even food, clothing, or shelter. North Philadelphia seemed an excellent section as the black population there was about six thousand. In addition, no other mission was to be found there except a Methodist one. On January 6th, 1878, the Session of Central Church which consisted of Dr. John B. Reeve, and Elders William Still and Robert Jones, with several lay members, organized the Gloucester Presbyterian Mission.

In conjunction with his regular church duties, William Still labored tirelessly with the Mission in the role of Superintendent of its Sabbath school. Many was the time he feared the Mission would fail. There were few active workers, and money was limited. But they carried on. Surprisingly, the Mission grew independent and survived.

Still also helped found a Y.M.C.A. Since whites and blacks disdained to mix socially, it was necessary for blacks to have their own. With his good friend, Reverend Phillips, William Still met with other interested people, and they formed a colored Y in 1880. Lewis Moore, a young black man, was placed in charge of the activities there, and until he left to become Dean of the Howard School of Education, he focused on the moral development of men and boys. Many pleasant hours were spent when he was in charge.

With Mr. Moore's departure, the committee which ran the Y selected a clergyman to replace him. Time proved that the minister was not equipped to do the work, as Reverend Phillips had surmised. For some reason he was un-

225

able to grasp the needs of the people. The work lagged. The project failed. The committee in charge complained and withheld their financial support.

Then a meeting was called at the Berean Presbyterian Church to consider the advisability of organizing an association for black people to borrow money to buy homes. Since it was very difficult for blacks to rent in any but the most dilapidated areas, it was desirable for them to buy their own houses on low terms. Since few had money, Still and his friends wanted an organization where black people could go to borrow money for this purpose. On the 12th of February, 1888, after an enthusiastic approval, the Berean Building and Loan Association was formed with William Still its first president.

Later, it was said: "There have been purchased through the Association since its organization, in 1888, two hundred and fifty homes for its stockholders, at an average valuation of $1,800, making the entire valuation of the homes owned now by the stockholders to be $450,000. . . . These two hundred and fifty homes are now for the most part excellently located on good streets, and it is quite possible that not one of them would have been purchased by these families had it not been for the assistance from the Association."

Although Reconstruction brought many changes in the activities of the Pennsylvania Anti-slavery Society, the interest William Still had in it had not diminished. The war was over. The slaves had been freed. Schools for their children had been established, and plans for their benefit had been enacted. All these events forced the members of the Society to question the advisability of any further efforts on behalf of the freedmen.

On September 10, 1864, a special meeting had been

called on the subject of closing the Anti-slavery office. Funds had diminished, and members wondered if it was even necessary to keep the office open. It seemed to them that only desk space was needed.

William Still offered his home to be used as an office for the Society. T. Ellwood Chapman, who lived at 5 South Fifth Street, offered his at seventy-five dollars a year. But Still's at 107 North Fifth was accepted when he offered it free of charge.

Even so, meetings were held farther and farther apart. At the meeting of the Executive Committee, held on May 3, 1870, they arranged a commemorative meeting, and decided to donate the books belonging to the Society to the Philadelphia Historical Society. The many volumes of the national *Anti-Slavery Standard* were promised to the Philadelphia Library.

On April 14th, 1875, the Society celebrated its hundredth anniversary. William Still presided at Concert Hall as Chairman of the Committee of Arrangements. Many eminent former abolitionists attended, such as the Honorable Henry Wilson, Vice President of the United States, Frederick Douglass, freed slave who became an ardent abolitionist, Lucretia Mott, antislavery woman and fighter for equal rights for women, Robert Purvis, of the old Vigilance Committee of the Abolition Society, and others. The Reverend W. H. Furness gave the invocation, and Henry Wilson delivered a commemorative oration eloquent in its appeal of sympathy for the work of the Society.

From the first day a white man aided a fugitive slave—which marked the real though unofficial start of the organization a century before—to the day that the remaining members met to bid it adieu, a world of change had occurred in the United States.

227

That this Society considered its work unfinished is shown by the minutes of a meeting following the Centennial. William Still read, at this time, a letter sent to him by a Mr. E. Webb, Financial Secretary of Lincoln University. Responding to its appeal for funds, the Society sent, upon motion, one hundred dollars as soon as they were able. They sent money to other black colleges, as well, including Wilberforce University, in Ohio.

As late as 1878, the Society was still in existence. Now they decided to leave a permanent record of their activities in the antislavery cause. After the publication of the third edition of Still's new book, now entitled, *Still's Underground Rail Road Records,* with a biographical sketch by James P. Boyd, in 1879, the Committee on Records asked to have the books of their organization properly labeled. The purpose was to compile a complete history of the Anti-slavery Society from its origin to the present, from its own records and manuscripts. They asked William S. Buck of the Historical Society to make selections of data to be incorporated into a history. The Committee on Records, composed of Dillwyn Parrish, Joseph M. Truman, and William Still, supervised this work. At this same time, Officers for the Boards of Education and the Acting Committee were selected. William Still was one of these.

The work of the Society continued as before, although general meetings were held only once a year. But the various board or committee meetings were held more often. Letters continued to arrive. In 1888, one was sent to them by Booker T. Washington, expressing appreciation for the "brave, generous, and unselfish work" of the Pennsylvania Anti-slavery Society.

William Still's interest continued. The Society undoubtedly appreciated his loyalty. He was voted in as Vice Presi--

dent from 1887 to 1895. And on December 26, 1895, he was elected President.

It was inevitable that the stress and strain of such a long, active life—crowded with so many unselfish deeds—would take its toll. His health began to fail, making it increasingly difficult to attend the meetings of his beloved Anti-slavery Society. After a while, he was unable to serve any longer.

The minutes explain what happened on April 25, 1901, when Howard Jenkins replaced the former President:

> A minute expressive of our appreciation on the extended services of our friend, William Still, as President of the Society, and of our regret at his extended condition of disability, was directed to be sent to him.
>
> Howard Jenkins,
Secretary

On July 14, 1902, William Still died at his home in Philadelphia. *The New York Times* reported that he was known throughout the country as "Father of the Underground Railroad," and although largely self-taught, was "one of the best educated members of the negro race." He left an estate valued at between $750,000 and $1,000,000, but far more extraordinary was his lifelong service to his fellow blacks, especially the poor, desperate fugitives who had come to him, seeking freedom via the Underground Railroad.

AN ANNOTATED BIBLIOGRAPHY

The Underground Rail Road by William Still was first published in 1872 by Porter and Coates in Philadelphia and went into several editions. The third edition contains a biographical sketch of William Still by James P. Boyd.

Early Life and Recollections by James Still, William's freeborn brother, was published by J. P. Lippincott in Philadelphia in 1877.

The Kidnapped and the Ransomed by Mrs. Kate Pickard is the story of Peter Still, William's brother, who was born in slavery. It was published in 1856 by E. O. Jenkins.

"Negro Welfare Work in Philadelphia Especially as Illustrated by the Career of William Still, 1875–1900," an unpublished master's thesis by Alberta S. Norwood (University of Pennsylvania, 1931), is the source of much of the material in Chapter 11. Miss Norwood interviewed Frances Still, William's daughter, who was alive at the time.

Other source material on William Still and his times can be found in the archives of the Historical Society of Pennsylvania, Friends Historical Library of Swarthmore College, Ohio Historical Society, and the New York Public Library.